matisse

henri matisse

john jacobus

Professor of Art, Dartmouth College

ABRAMS, NEW YORK

1   **Dance** 1909
   Oil on canvas, 96 ⅝ x 153 ⅝ in.
   Museum of Modern Art, New York City
   Gift of Governor Nelson A. Rockefeller in honor of Alfred H. Barr, Jr.

Contents

henri
matisse

The world that Henri Matisse left behind at his death on November 3, 1954, was vastly changed from that which had initially sustained his talent in the Paris of the 1890s. At the time the undisputed art capital of the Western world, that city of the belle époque would surely strike us today as parochial if not provincial. The Parisian art world was still, on the eve of the twentieth century, inward-oriented, self-contained, and largely unconcerned with events elsewhere. There existed numerous coteries, ranging from traditional to radical, that claimed their various supporters. For at least a century Paris had been an international magnet, a focus drawing artists from all over the world, and it was, in fact, destined to play that unique role for another quarter century. Center of a strict and hierarchical academic establishment, the Paris of the nineteenth century had nonetheless nourished a rapid succession of revolutionary movements in the visual arts, and, in 1900, some of its finest moments had yet to be acted out. It was this milieu that Matisse, born in a small town in the north of France on the last day of the old year, 1869, entered when he came to Paris as an aspiring art student in the autumn of 1891, at the age of twenty-two. He was a late starter, having previously begun a career in law, which he had studied in Paris in 1887–88. At first without knowledge of the new tendencies in painting, he sought, though with reluctance, to become a student of Adolphe Bouguereau, one of the lionized academic luminaries of the day—only to find himself denied official acceptance to the École des Beaux-Arts. Discovered by a less hidebound master, the gentle Gustave Moreau, he was invited to join that painter's atelier in 1892. Over the next decade and more, Matisse would very gradually discover the new movements in French painting, progressing steadily but with great deliberation, selecting, rejecting, and then returning to various new tendencies as he sought to find himself as a painter.

Throughout his long career, Matisse's art was nourished and replenished by a variety of nineteenth-century movements: Neoclassicism, Realism, Impressionism, and Post Impressionism, though not necessarily in that order. As a whole, Matisse's style is inconceivable and inexplicable without this tradition, and yet he developed into one of the most inventive of twentieth-century masters, one of the few painters of the first half of the century who continue to have a major influence on the younger painters of today. Matisse's artistic roots were pronouncedly Parisian, and yet his late works thoroughly transcended this stylistic locale. They became a major influence on the international art culture of the later twentieth century to a degree that is not remotely equaled by some of the other masters of the School of Paris: painters as different as Braque and Bonnard, who, like

1

Matisse, were also concerned with the sensuous transformation into pigment of an optically perceived reality, no matter how different their individual stylistic affiliations might be.

In this respect, Matisse's art moves beyond the restricted ambiance of such close personal friends as the painters Marquet, Camoin, and Bonnard, men whose art was primarily directed toward the winding up and completion of a particular vision inherited from the past. In the larger sense, Matisse's career instead must be seen as parallel to the quests of those like his non-Parisian contemporaries, notably Kandinsky and Mondrian. Both of these artists had started at roughly the same point in time and style, although in different national traditions. More swiftly than Matisse, they transcended the materialistic realism of the late nineteenth century, and, in a political sense, went further into the worlds of abstract and nonobjective painting. With Matisse, the struggle to transcend the world of visual perception was much more time consuming, painstaking, and even poignant. He remained to his last days committed to the pictorial transformation of the world of appearances, creating works that were untroubled with systematic metaphysical speculation, works that yet remain pregnant with the germ of a new spirit, works that still serve as a key foundation for the new abstraction and even the new realism of the later twentieth century.

Matisse's nominal historical position was as leader of the Fauves, just as Picasso and, to an extent, Braque would be considered the leaders of the Cubists. However, Fauvism was a fragile, short-lived movement, one which never possessed a formulated program, not even after the fact. Of all the Fauves, it was only Matisse who went on to still greater achievements in the direction of intense though simplified color harmonies and refined draftsmanship. His contacts with Albert Marquet, beginning as early as 1892; with Andre Derain, in 1899; and subsequently with the other painters who were grouped together in the "cage of wild beasts" at the 1905 Autumn Salon—Maurice de Vlaminck, Georges Rouault, and others—certainly served to reinforce Matisse's own commitment to bold color effects. However, the group seems to have coalesced more through the coincidences of several personal tastes than out of the development of a common program for a new painting. Probably Matisse gained as much if not more from his study of old masters in the Louvre, from his preoccupations with Cézanne, Gauguin, and other recent masters, and his personal encounters with such older painters as Pissarro, Signac, and Cross. If Fauvism had not existed as a movement around 1905, it probably would have made very little difference in the overall development of Matisse's art. Sadly, most of his Fauve associates have been gradually eclipsed in reputation over the years, largely because they failed to sustain much of their initial promise. Some, it is true, were hardly more than belated Impressionists, but others, like Derain, were painters of considerable talent and intelligence who, in later career, were tempted into a traditionalism that lacked the mark of individuality and adventure found in the work of Matisse.

Matisse's nominal rival through most of his career was Picasso. Significantly, the two artists preserved a cautious friendship, together with a profound respect for each other's works, for a half century. They even exhibited together in 1945, and at an early date their works were avidly collected by the same people: Gertrude Stein and her relatives; their friends the Misses Cone; Dr. Albert C. Barnes; and the two Muscovites Sergei Shchukin and Ivan Morosov. It is, however, interesting to reflect that while Matisse's final works foreshadow art movements that were yet to be born at the moment of his death in 1954, Picasso at that juncture was paradoxically embarking on a long retrospective dialogue with the past, commencing a reflective study of specific works by Delacroix, Velázquez, Manet, and others, a sustained project that also embraced themes from his earlier work.

The multiple and often contradictory trajectories of these two long careers frequently intersect, and we can even detect exchanges of admiration in certain pictures, where one of them develops and reinterprets a theme previously explored by the other. However, their points of departure and of culmination were curiously alien, even though they shared, each in his own way, certain serious interests: the interpretation of the human face and figure; the specific environmental quality of the artist's studio; and, in some of their more ambitious compositions, deeply personal attitudes concerning the human condition, either as it exists or as it ought ideally to exist.

More than any other twentieth-century painter, Matisse's total oeuvre, seen in its gradual unfolding, appears as a logical continuation of earlier quests: specifically, those that reach back to Poussin, Chardin, Watteau, Courbet, Manet, and Cézanne. The emphasis here is on "continuation." He consulted these masters frequently, but they were not so much objects of passive meditation as springboards for his own restless, ongoing search for a style that was uniquely his, one which never remained static but was always growing and maturing, deviating but never changing essential direction from beginning to end, even as it approached abstraction. Moreover, his growth appears more inwardly consistent than that of Picasso, who alone among his contemporaries would be able to outdistance him in the richness of stylistic variation. Unlike the more mercurial Picasso, Matisse as a young artist studied the great masters with painstaking care, postponing his nominal "graduation" from student ranks. Hence, in later career he had less need of extensive renewal from the past; indeed, he was able to turn to traditional styles in his later years with less self-consciousness, with results that were constructive rather than disruptive to his inner growth.

Picasso's early work indicates an impulsive prodigy, a sensibility that absorbed lessons with incredible speed. Matisse's beginnings were altogether different, rather plodding, never pedestrian but occasionally pedantic. He saw to it that his base in the traditions of his chosen craft was solid almost to excess. His earliest original paintings tend to be still lifes (though he did produce academic figure drawings at that time), and only slowly did he expand, first to landscape and then to major figure paintings. Throughout his career he remained devoted to these three genres, frequently combining them as the principal themes of his life gradually emerged. Each of the primary genres—still life, landscape, and figure composition—would appear, their roles and importance constantly shifting, in his lifelong quest to record and transform on canvas the appearance of the artist's habitual environment, the studio. In effect, Matisse conducted a private dialogue between himself and his working space together with its contents: models, other works of art, and

2 **Study for Girl in Green** 1921
Pencil, 12 x 9 1/2 in.
Collection Mr. and Mrs. Ralph F. Colin, New York

3 **Girl in Green** 1921
Oil on canvas, 25 1/2 x 21 1/2 in.
Collection Mr. and Mrs. Ralph F. Colin, New York

2

3

those inanimate objects whose sole purpose was to stimulate the creation of the pictorial image. In a literal, representational way, the majority of his works were comments on the creative process, and hence certain of his pictures are professionally as well as personally autobiographical. They describe not the artist's personal sentimental feelings about other humans (as is so often the case in Picasso's pictures devoted to the subject of the artist and model), but rather manifest the artist's efforts to create an autonomous pictorial life in each individual work.

Matisse's unremitting concern with his profession is visible even in the major paintings of his family seen as a group, where his wife and children are frequently placed in close association with his other offspring, his paintings and sculptures. Matisse never went to the tendentious extreme of Courbet, whose enormous **Atelier** (1854–55) sought, with a single gesture, to recount the artist's personal and professional encounters over a period of several years, with an allegorical telescoping of time and space. In Matisse's treatment of the studio, sometimes no more than a temporarily inhabited hotel room, the artist is often unseen, or if he is actually present, his position is marginal, fractional, sometimes coming only in a mirror reflection. He wished not to stress the central, heroic role of the artist in the midst of his struggles, but rather to indicate his fleeting presence, leaving the work itself as the only possible hero. He intended his work to reflect a state of balance and repose in its completed form when it was finally ready for contemplation by the spectator. He did not wish it to express the often strenuous effort which he, the artist, had put into its creation as a matter of professional problem solving. The layman is thus meant to be excluded from the artist's world of tensions, uncertainties, and triumphs, but is instead offered a completed work which, in Matisse's hope, would have a calming, evocative effect that would serve to lift the beholder beyond the limits of his own mundane experience. It is almost as if he were implying that the life and goals of the artist at work could serve as a model for those engaged in other pursuits.

Not only did Matisse employ his studio as a constant motif, but he had a vision of how an artist's studio should be decorated. While many of his early paintings suggest the customary working interior, with its haphazard collection of objects of varying source and value, by 1909 he had reached a more elaborate, mature view, one that featured his own paintings as a major part of a carefully conceived ensemble. Contemporary with his negotiations with the Russian collector Sergei Shchukin,

4

which resulted ultimately in **Dance** and **Music** (pages 73 and 75), he conceived a parallel scheme for an imaginary studio of his own which he explained to a journalist acquaintance, Estienne, in the spring of 1909. Matisse imagined a three-story studio in which **Dance** ("something calling at once for an effort and also giving a feeling of relaxation") would dominate the ground level. "On the second floor we are in the heart of the house, where all is silence, pensive meditation. Here I picture a scene of music making with attentive listeners." In truth, the listeners vanished from **Music** in the hieratic, almost symbolic version delivered to Shchukin, but the contrast with the effort and energy of **Dance** is still unmistakable. "Then, on the third floor, all is peace; I paint some people lying on the grass, engaged in talk or lost in dreams" (*Les Nouvelles*, April 12, 1909). In actuality, this third panel, markedly changed from its original design, emerged as **Bathers by the River**, completed only in 1916–17 (page 97). While Matisse's concepts as outlined here are partly inconsistent with respect to

expressive and psychological mood, they indicate a desire to convert his studio into an artful paradise, to create an ambiance relying upon calculated figure compositions to establish a state of mind that would lead to further creative effort. The very fact that Matisse painted and kept in his studio a full-size study for **Dance** (frontispiece)—its left margin visible at the extreme right of **Pink Studio** (page 79) and appearing as the backdrop for other works of the period—is indicative that this journalistic account was more than a fleeting fantasy. Indeed, it helps explain the sequence of monumental studio varia-tions over the next few years, and predicts the way in which he converted his various temporary residences in Nice during the 1920s into uniquely calculated pictorial environments—a phenomenon that is amply demonstrated in **Moorish Screen** (figure 33)—through the use of carefully assembled objects and fabrics that overwhelm the ordinary models.

The themes of dancers and musicians and of "people lying on the grass, engaged in talk or lost in dreams," all

5 **Interior with Top Hat** 1896
Oil on canvas, 31½ x 37⅜ in.
Collection M. and Mme Georges Duthuit, Paris

6 **Studio of Gustave Moreau** 1894–95
Oil on canvas, 25⅝ x 31⅞ in.
Private collection, Paris

5

6

emerged from his seminal masterpiece of 1906, **Joy of Life** (figure 4, page 65), an arcadian composition that not only marked his apogee as a Fauve but pointed the way beyond. Together with the Neo-Impressionist **Luxe, calme et volupté** of the previous season (page 59), this painting set the stage for a series of even more monumental figure studies that would ultimately lead Matisse to transform his previously realistic image of the artist's studio. These paintings would turn it into a world inhabited by detached, uninvolved models serving as the passive consorts of beautifully shaped or textured inanimate objects. With these two calculated "masterpieces" of the period 1905–6, both painted in his Paris studio after studies made in the south of France, he established contact with the nearly lost tradition of mythological "Golden Age" paintings which had been central to the works of Titian, Poussin, and Watteau, not to mention such late nineteenth-century masters as Puvis de Chavannes and even, in a special sense, Gauguin. Very few twentieth-century painters have joined Matisse in the perpetuation of the vision of a terrestrial paradise populated by gods in human guise, or humans in godlike attitudes. In projecting his imaginary studio and in working out the actual decorative canvases of **Dance** and **Music** for Shchukin, the artist had achieved a significant fusion of two elements in his work. He had found that the visions of a mythological harmony that he had expressed again and again in his large figure compositions of 1905–10 could be expressively (and not just anecdotally) incorporated in his studio concept, a theme that reached back to his dark pictures dating from before 1900. Stretching a point, it might be contended that the whole of his subsequent work is predicated upon this illuminating insight.

Matisse's early paintings of the studio motif were, in effect, expanded still lifes, and only gradually did the live model intrude. A case in point is the **Interior with Top Hat** (figure 5). It is clear that we are here looking at a corner of the artist's studio. The hat itself is something of a decoy, since the majority of the objects are pictures, frames, and stretchers hanging on or stacked against the wall. The tones of the picture are essentially somber, and evoke memories of his very earliest painting, **Books and Candle** (1890; Musée Matisse, Nice-Cimiez), a picture painted before he had returned to Paris as an art student the following year. As with most of the still lifes of this period, we are face to face with an emerging talent which quickly and instinctively mastered the art of composing traditionally arranged objects on a table or seen against a wall in a realistic manner. It is not surprising, therefore, to discover that some of his early copies after old masters were works in this genre by Chardin and Jan de Heem, and that some of his original compositions of this period appear as pastiches in the manner of Courbet and Manet. In short, he was beginning his personal statement as an artist (even though he was still a student) in a style that, by avant-garde standards of the 1890s, was already outmoded. Ironically, however, this realism was hardly acceptable to the artist who was—briefly and, we must suppose, grudgingly—his master at the Académie Julian, the academic hero of the day, Adolphe Bouguereau. Unwittingly, Matisse was, in his early work, caught among several extremes: the novel color and composition of Synthetist and Nabi painting which at that point constituted one advanced extreme of Parisian art; the fashionable Art Nouveau style; and the sentimentally frigid Classicism of the admired Salon masters.

7 **La Desserte** 1897
Oil on canvas, 39 1/2 x 51 1/2 in.
Collection Mr. and Mrs. Stavros Niarchos, Paris

7

As yet he was barely aware of new tendencies, but his instincts led him to recoil from the banality of academic work or from something so immediately popular and transient as Art Nouveau.

His pencil studies of the live model dating from the early 1890s (figure 8), or alternatively of antique plaster casts, are strongly outlined and crisply linear. However, in detail we sense a conflict between certain contours that are of a realistic definition and others that suggest an effort to approach the codes of academic idealization. In any case, these drawings were not to the liking of Bouguereau, and Matisse was refused formal admission to the École des Beaux-Arts. Luckily he was discovered sketching on his own in the courtyard of the École by the more open Gustave Moreau, and was invited to become an unofficial student in the latter's atelier, where he worked, off and on, with time out for trips to Brittany and the south of France, until after Moreau's death in 1898. With Moreau's encouragement he copied works of a variety of masters in the Louvre—a learning method that was considered novel for the day. Moreau did not impose his own distinctive style and taste upon Matisse, or upon his other pupils, for that matter, but encouraged them to study life around them as well as the paintings hanging in the museum. Moreau's own manner, traceable ultimately to Delacroix, with his mordant symbolic themes featuring a rich tapestry of slender, languid figures, seems to have had little bearing on Matisse's personal style either then or later. It is not out of the question, however, that Matisse, in his large allegorical figure compositions of 1905–10, was reacting, in his striking simplicity of strong color and contour, to the overburdened detail and affectedly flaccid design of Moreau's suggestively erotic scenes.

In any event, Matisse's painting **Studio of Gustave Moreau** (figure 6) is a rare picture of the period which

8 **Classical Study** 1890–92
   Graphite, 24 3/8 x 18 1/2 in.
   Musée Matisse, Nice-Cimiez

9 **The Abduction of Rebecca, after Delacroix** 1899
   Ink

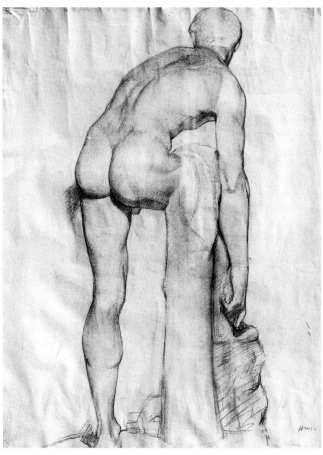

8

9

demonstrates his determination to treat the human figure with the same somber realism that he had already mastered in his still lifes. The live model, backlit, dominates the central foreground, and in the right distance a standard studio prop, an antique plaster cast of a standing figure, is caught in a highlight. It is unimaginable that such open brushwork and emphatic realism would have been tolerated in any other atelier of the day. The somber hues indicate that Matisse was not interested in the often fervid colors in Moreau's own work, and, in fact, the liberation of his palette would take place not in the studio but in the face of nature itself, during his summer trips to Brittany in 1895–97. Even then the process appears to have been a slow, gradual one and not the result of a sudden revelation. His discovery of the new, postrealist art movements was slow, almost as if, in a period of several years, he was reliving the history of the past thirty years in his own work. During the later nineties, however, he did not neglect his study of the masters in the Louvre either, and in 1896 he exhibited publicly for the first time. Significantly, he presented his work neither at the official Salon nor at the Salon des Indépendants, frequently the scene of exhibition for radical artists from Seurat onward

(and where Matisse would exhibit his Neo-Impressionist **Luxe, calme et volupté** in 1905). Instead, reflecting the caution of his art at the time and his middle-of-the-road position, he submitted four works to the Salon of the Société Nationale des Beaux-Arts, whose president at that time was Puvis de Chavannes, and they were accepted. The Société Nationale had separated itself a few years previously from the official Salon, and had originally been headed by the renowned genre painter Meissonier. Since it did not look with favor on radical innovations but was receptive to individual efforts of a modest or stylish sort (Sargent, Boldini, and Carolus-Duran exhibited here), this was an appropriate place for Matisse to make his public debut. His success was such that the state purchased **Woman Reading** (page 49). But the following year a more ambitious and daringly hued picture, **La Desserte** (figure 7), was poorly received. This picture, undertaken with the encouragement of Gustave Moreau, who felt that his student was ready for a large-scale effort, marks the beginning of a long transitional period in Matisse's art, one that would not end until his Fauve paintings of 1905. In effect, it was the second phase of his prolonged student effort, one which witnessed his initiation into various aspects of modernist

10 **The Slave** 1900–03
Bronze, 36 1/8 in. high
Baltimore Museum of Art, Cone Collection

11 **The Model (Nu aux Souliers Roses)** 1900
Oil on canvas, 29 1/2 x 22 7/8 in.
Collection G. Daelemans, Brussels

10

11

painting. Yet it was also a period in which the artist swung back and forth between daring color experiments and a return to the darker palette of his very first paintings, albeit with a command of compositional structure that reached far beyond the modest, if limitedly successful, efforts of his earliest works. This period would also witness his beginnings as a sculptor, and, toward its end, his first tentative efforts as a printmaker.

La Desserte is an intriguing picture, mixing boldness of touch and novelty of viewpoint (the spectator is looking down upon a luncheon table from a very close vantage) with a certain conventionality. It lacks the sense of release from the realist tradition that would appear in the Corsican and Toulouse landscapes of 1898, and in many respects it is not as satisfactory a picture as several of the cliffside views painted at Belle-Île during his last Breton summer, 1897. While many of the details of **La Desserte** are exquisitely rendered with a genuine luminosity, the composition is overloaded and the density of the pigment is uneven, tending to pile up more heavily toward the center of the picture. And if there is an impressionistic sense of sparkle emanating from the objects on the cloth at the center, there is also a rather compromising

lugubriousness in the colors of the periphery. Nonetheless, it remains an important landmark in Matisse's early career, and the picture's contradictions clearly indicate the struggle that he was undergoing at the time. In his later works we rarely see the conflicts and dilemmas faced by the artist in the process of creating a picture, but here they are in full view.

By 1898, Matisse had commenced his integration into the mainstream of contemporary art. He had encountered Impressionism the previous year through the appearance of the truncated Caillebotte legacy at the Luxembourg Museum, and had been introduced to Pissarro, who was then painting some of his most luminous late Impressionist views of Paris from the upper-floor windows of various buildings, rounding out his career with a series of paintings that returned in touch and sensibility to the pioneering Impressionist works of the 1870s. No doubt these works would challenge Matisse over the next few years as he studied alternately Notre-Dame and the Pont Saint Michel from his upper-floor studio window overlooking the quais of the left bank. It was Pissarro who encouraged Matisse to visit London in order to see the work of Turner, a trip that the older master had made during

1870–71, as had Monet. The trip was a prelude to a long voyage that would keep Matisse away from Paris for most of 1898. Nothing in his subsequent work is directly indebted to the English Romantic master, but this totally new experience with a kind of painting that could not have been seen in Paris may have provided a necessary jolt which permitted his next phase to develop with extraordinary freedom.

The paintings that Matisse produced during 1898, in Corsica and then in the environs of Toulouse, give us the first clear indication of his uniqueness. Powerfully rich in color, small in scale, and boldly brushed, they are free of the understandable inhibitions that grew out of a Parisian atelier ambiance. Justifiably, they have been called Proto-Fauve. Almost exclusively landscapes, they threatened to turn the direction and emphasis of Matisse's career toward that of the Impressionists themselves, but their stepped-up, highly personal hues precluded that route. However, it is clear from the evidence of the paintings and of Matisse's own later testimony that his taste for Mediterranean light was first established at this time. True, twenty years later, when he began his habitual winter sojourns on the Riviera, he was more preoccupied with the subtle nuances created by this limpid light in interiors; but during his first protracted experience with the sun of the south of France he was bewitched by its intense exterior dazzle. Free of the internal politics and the competitive hassle of an art capital, Matisse here gave vent to lyrical feelings that would ripen a decade later in larger, more disciplined, and more ambitious canvases. He was even able to transfer some of his newfound enthusiasm for rendering light by means of intensified juxtapositions of saturated colors to an occasional interior study.

Matisse returned to Paris early in the year 1899, and his stylistic development entered a series of troubled perplexing phases. The easy flow of minor but satisfactorily personal pictures ended, though not abruptly. His discovery of Cézanne at this juncture (he purchased Cézanne's **Three Bathers** from Vollard at this time) almost certainly demonstrated to him that his days of study were not yet over, that there were works by contemporary painters that he needed to study meticulously before he could embark on a career entirely his own. Regrettably his master, Gustave Moreau, had died in his absence. Fernand Cormon, the academic painter who subsequently took over Moreau's studio, dismissed Matisse on the flimsy pretext that he was over-age, and the artist had to find other working quarters. To complicate matters, his interests were acquiring still other, somewhat contradictory dimensions: he came under the influence of Signac and of Neo-Impressionism through a reading of *De Eugène Delacroix au Néo-Impressionnisme*, which had appeared serially in the *Revue Blanche* in 1898, during his

12

absence, and was issued in book form in the following year. Quite possibly it was while under its spell that he made his pen-and-ink study of Delacroix's **Abduction of Rebecca** (figure 9), which, according to Jean Puy, a fellow student and future Fauve, produced consternation because it seemed to reverse the scale of values, replacing highlights with shadows and vice versa. This observation is in fact exaggerated. Matisse's aim with this study was to provide the figures with a greater sense of relief by surrounding them with extraordinarily broad, overstated shadows. What emerged was a style of drawing that would prove to be the black-and-white equivalent of Fauve painting and, consequently, perhaps the most important study that the artist ever made from the works of a recognized master.

In rapid succession to his involvement in the theory and practice of Neo-Impressionism (there are loosely conceived paintings in this mode which may even have been painted during his last weeks in Toulouse in early 1899), Matisse abruptly became interested in the problems of three-dimensional modeling posed by the art of sculpture. He had purchased a Rodin bust from Vollard at the same time that

13 **Blue Nude, Souvenir de Biskra** 1907
Oil on canvas, 36 1/4 x 55 1/8 in.
Baltimore Museum of Art, Cone Collection

13

he acquired Cézanne's **Three Bathers**, and an inconclusive meeting with Rodin took place shortly thereafter. Such concerns with modeling would somehow seem altogether contradictory to his interest in the diaphanous space and surface of Neo-Impressionist painting as manifested in its mosaic of dots or short brush marks. Moreover, both concerns appear foreign to the lyrical flow of brushwork and design of his immediately preceding Toulouse landscapes. However, it is out of such contradictory concerns that Matisse was forging the foundations of his career around 1900. None of these experiences were capricious adventures; all proved useful as his work ripened over the next decade. Indeed, the great "blue" nude studies of 1900, notably the **Male Model** (page 51), suggest that he was already prepared to fuse the lessons of Cézanne and Rodin into a work totally his own. As for Neo-Impressionism, its ultimate consequences would not be felt until 1904–5, when Matisse had the opportunity of meeting Signac in person.

At this crucial moment in his development, poised on the brink of establishing a definitive artistic personality, economic circumstances were partly responsible for a certain contraction and retreat. In order to make ends meet he was forced (together with his close friend Marquet) to work as a day laborer on the decorations of the Grand Palais, then being rushed to completion for the World's Fair of 1900, and during 1902 he was obliged to return for a time to his family's home in Bohain. Grim though this period must have been, it resulted in the unheralded **Attic Studio** (page 55), in which the theme and format of so much of his life's work would be tentatively announced in a style that was still not free of early dark tendencies, but one which showed little evidence of the strenuous, seemingly contradictory interests of the preceding twenty-four months.

Ever since the mid–nineties he had been making acquaintance with artists who would ultimately form the Fauve contingent at the 1905 Autumn Salon. Some of these were fellow students from the Moreau atelier, the most important of whom was Albert Marquet, eventually Matisse's neighbor at 19 Quai Saint-Michel. He did not meet André Derain until 1899, during a brief stay in Carrière's studio, and through

14

him came to know Maurice de Vlaminck. Marquet surely reinforced his impulse to make many studies of Notre-Dame through his studio window, several of which are clearly Proto-Fauve, but the major tendency of Matisse's art from 1900 to 1903 was toward a drying-up of color, until he had passed the important stage of tight compositional study marked by **Carmelina** in 1903 (page 57). The design density of this, one of his most conservative and traditional works, was a significant catharsis, a self-verification that he had mastered the foundations of his craft. His self-imposed, prolonged apprenticeship was nearing its end; it had, in fact, but one further step to take. This involved a return to a more receptive attitude toward primary colors in their full intensity. For this to come about, a return to a Mediterranean atmosphere was necessary, and the means were put at Matisse's disposal by Signac and Henri-Edmond Cross during the summer of 1904 at Saint-Tropez. This period witnessed a notable revival of Neo-Impressionist painting, and in particular the work of Cross was reinvigorated at about this time by a switch in subject matter. Where earlier he had been concerned with rural,

peasant subjects, he now began to employ more arcadian themes, with landscapes populated by nude figures in recreational attitudes along sunlit shores. Matisse fell in with this motif and also with a luminosity of style that had been absent from his works for several years. The first study for **Luxe, calme et volupté** was executed during this stay at Saint-Tropez, in a fairly open, loose style that was not yet Neo-Impressionist in a doctrinaire fashion. From this preestablished image he executed the final version in Paris during the winter of 1904-5, and it was subsequently shown at the Salon des Indépendants that spring. Signac was so sure that he had made a major convert to his style from the ranks of gifted younger artists that he immediately purchased the picture—only to discover a little more than a year later that in fact Matisse had been using this technique as a momentary vehicle leading to the discovery of his own proper idiom.

However, it was actually across the bridge of a momentarily revived Neo-Impressionism that Matisse, and also Derain (who had accompanied him to Saint-Tropez in 1904), found their road to Fauvism. It was a course of development

15 **Reclining Nude I** 1907
Bronze 13½ in. high
The Museum of Modern Art, New York
The Lillie P. Bliss Bequest

16 **Goldfish** 1909
Oil on canvas, 32¼ x 36¾ in.
The Royal Museum of Fine Arts, Copenhagen
J. Rump Collection

15

16

that differed from that of Vlaminck, whose use of saturated color had been more daring, even unwise, and still different from the road to be followed by Dufy and Braque. Interestingly, Dufy later confessed that seeing **Luxe, calme et volupté** had served to disenchant him with whatever lingering Impressionism remained in his work at that time.

The meticulous working out of this Cythera-like theme in Matisse's work served as a prologue for his breakthrough into a personally evolved Fauvism during his stay at Collioure during the summer of 1905. Several Neo-Impressionist canvases were painted there, but their mosaic-like effect was transformed into something more vibrant in the **Open Window, Collioure** (page 63), with its broad, continuously painted patches of saturated color. After this achievement the road was open, leading to the two portraits of Mme. Matisse, **Woman with the Hat** (Collection Mr. and Mrs. Walter A. Haas) and **The Green Stripe** (page 61), which were painted upon his return to Paris in the fall. Exhibited together in a single room in the Autumn Salon of that year, together with equally challenging works by Derain, Rouault, Henri Manguin, Jean Puy, and Louis Valtat, the eclipse of Signac's systematic mode was definitive. Fauvism's unique if transitory Indian summer of the old Impressionistic vision had coalesced into a communal celebration of color created by a group of artists working not so much in concert as in parallel, developing an art movement of brief duration out of overlapping but not exactly consonant enthusiasms.

Luxe, calme et volupté established the theme, and the smaller Fauve canvases of middle and late 1905 clarified the new style. The result was **Joy of Life** (figure 4), the most prescient, far-reaching single effort that Matisse ever made. In its final, monumental form it appeared at the Salon des Indépendants in 1906, though its original conception would seem to reach back to studies made from nature at Collioure the previous summer. Frontal rather than diagonal in its spatial organization, with bolder liberties taken with space-scale relationships, and featuring flat planes of color rather than a pseudo-atmospheric assemblage of mosaic-like, staccato brush strokes, Matisse's art here achieved a harmony of style and theme which established his independence as an artist capable of working on a vast scale and in a decorative style that already bears a hint of architectural aspirations. Far and away the largest canvas that he had attempted up to this point (its dimensions exceeding five and a half by seven and a half feet), its design was a model of balance and clarity, and the control of its dense color a demonstration of the artist's emotional response to a hallowed, traditional arcadian theme, an emotion tempered by intellectual restraint. Not only the source of several subsequent works, **Joy of Life** is the fulcrum of his early career and the necessary preliminary summation of the complex, unified urges that would drive his painting forward for another half century.

18

17

The calming atmosphere of this rich yet sparsely designed canvas appears to have put aright the tortured, unresolved fantasies of his teacher, Gustave Moreau, while solving, in a unified set of gestures, the inner tensions and contradictions of his own work of the previous years. Ironically, it may have been the unusual size of the picture's format that was the key; ironically because in the past, in some of his more ambitious early works, notably **La Desserte** (figure 7) nearly a decade before, it seems to have been the scale of his ambitions that in the end precluded a total success. With **Joy of Life** the possibilities of decorative gesture provoked by mere size seem to have unlocked a tendency that was, in the next five years, destined to expand still further in his most monumental figurative works. One can only conclude that at last, after much deliberate and cautious preparation, Matisse was ready to set forth on his own. In so doing he became the last member of a race of painters whose genealogy stretches back to Titian and his older contemporaries, Bellini and Giorgione, and which reaches the twentieth century through the classicizing figurative compositions of Cézanne and Renoir. And yet, in spite of these unmistakable historical affiliations (which were probably only half conscious in the artist's mind at the moment of creation), this is a painting that clearly speaks in a language of the twentieth century. While the theme of **Joy of Life** was universal and idyllic, its style was not only new but susceptible to yet more growth

and intensification. Its linking of past and present is in every respect reminiscent of Manet's **Déjeuner sur l'herbe** (1863). The psychic and erotic tensions that Cézanne had brought to subjects of this sort, or the sentimentality that Renoir infused into his treatments of similar motifs, are here eliminated. Out of this objective balance of forces, one rivaling the equilibrium of Poussin or Ingres, Matisse found his true métier as a poet.

The ensuing half decade saw Matisse working in a variety of genres: still life, interior, portrait, and landscape. Moreover, it was the period of several great early bronzes: **Reclining Nude I** (figure 15) and **La Serpentine** (figure 26). However, the most significant creations of this period of early maturity were the large figure compositions, several of which were in effect clarifying "blowups" or monumental condensations of themes taken from **Joy of Life**. This series led through the two versions of **Le Luxe** (figure 19, page 67), and culminated in the **Dance** and **Music** of 1910 (pages 73 and 75). Then, abruptly, as if his appetite for the grouping of human figures were exhausted, the key expressive position in Matisse's art was given to the great studio allegories of 1911–12.

The direction followed by Matisse in the years after 1906 is exceptional from many points of view. Unlike his Fauve friends, he seems not to have flirted seriously with the then nascent Cubist techniques. He appears to have been determined to solve the problem of modeling a figure simultaneously with the creation of a sturdy decorative rhythm of line and

19 **Le Luxe II** 1907
   Casein, 82 1/2 x 54 3/4 in.
   The Royal Museum of Fine Arts, Copenhagen
   J. Rump Collection

20 **Music (Sketch)** 1907
   Oil on canvas, 28 3/4 x 23 5/8 in.
   The Museum of Modern Art, New York
   Gift of A. Conger Goodyear in honor of Alfred H. Barr, Jr.

19

20

a powerful contrast of large, flat areas of color and value. His goal was perhaps similar to that of the Cubists, but his means were totally opposite (the goal being the reconciliation of two inherently contradictory problems: to provide, if not literally an illusion, at least a sense of volume for the figure represented, while at the same time maintaining the integrity of the canvas's surface through overall design). That Matisse was convinced of his own personal methods at this point saved him from the crisis that overtook many of his contemporaries when they first encountered Cubism. Of the Fauves, only Braque contributed to the new movement, one that many must have seen as a rival for leadership to the barely established Fauvist group. For the rest, Derain, Dufy, and even de Vlaminck, after testing out certain of the constructive lessons of Cézanne in ways that might be called Proto-Cubist in the years 1907–10, returned to either a neotraditionalist eclecticism based upon various nineteenth-century achievements

or to a fashionable accommodation to bourgeois taste. Their later work was often skilled, but it was outside the mainstream.

In effect, Matisse was the only Fauve who derived lasting benefit from the movement's unique dedication to saturated color. His entire career is predicated upon refining this investigation, which was tentatively begun in his small landscapes of 1898, momentarily put aside, only to be reformulated in a more definitive fashion in 1905. His concern for color was always closely integrated with his preoccupation with suggestions of depth and of relief in or upon the canvas: in other words, the problems of spatial illusion and bodily modeling. His effort in pulling together into a single formula all of these needs and urges generated much tension in his work in 1907. A comparison of the **Blue Nude, Souvenir de Biskra** (figure 13) and **Le Luxe I** and **II** is instructive. The reclining blue figure is ponderous, muscular, earthbound, with the woman surrounded by a lush landscape fragment that serves

21 **Five Bathers (Composition II)**
First study for Bathers by the River 1910
Pen, ink, brush, aquarelle, 8 1/2 x 11 3/8 in.
Pushkin Museum, Moscow

21

to press the figure forward, heightening the sense of tactile volume to an unusual extreme, while also echoing, in its design, the simple decorative contours of the body's outline. Contrary to this is the decorative etherealization that has taken place with the major figures of **Le Luxe I** and **II** and their relationship to a landscape, which is established through contrast rather than repetition. In effect, **Le Luxe I** is the canvas in which the transition from a ponderous to a contoured figure can still be seen, the artist having left this work as an indication of his personal struggles. **Blue Nude** (whose subtitle refers to a trip to Algeria the previous year) may be considered a late Fauve work by virtue of its forceful, complex palette. In contrast, **Le Luxe II** opens the way to a period of harmony—of simplified yet powerful forms and color contrasts.

   Blue Nude's impact is clarified through a comparison with the bronze **Reclining Nude I** (figure 15), a work that is

often the subject in subsequent paintings of the next decade, being transformed finally into a garden figure in the 1917 **Music Lesson** (figure 31). But in spite of the fact that color is here used to heighten the sense of relief, working in concert with the massive outlines and exaggerated shadows above and below the torso, one can still detect the latent linear arabesques underneath. This phenomenon points toward the distant as well as the near future of Matisse's art, and an examination of **Pink Nude** (figure 14), like **Blue Nude** also a part of the Cone Collection, in conjunction with its Fauve predecessor points out the inner unity of the artist's development across a long period of time. These two works seen together underline the evolutionary growth of his style through the apprehension and presentation of the female figure. Indeed, the **Pink Nude**, a picture whose pose and rather Ingresque proportions were arrived at only after many trials and modifications, ends up as an almost mirrorlike

22

23

reinterpretation of the **Blue Nude**, painted nearly three decades earlier.

The two versions of **Le Luxe** likewise illustrate Matisse's tenacity in developing a particular theme or figure type over a protracted period. **Le Luxe** thematically emerges as a less episodic, more monumental treatment of the earlier **Luxe, calme et volupté**. These are essentially bathing compositions, and one senses motifs in both that might have been borrowed or transformed from Cézanne and Gauguin. But Matisse, unlike all his Parisian contemporaries, finally chose to emphasize the latent arabesque rather than to concentrate upon the constructive, volumetric aspects that are constantly present in the compositions of Cézanne. It is here that Matisse parts company not only with the Fauves but also with those who would shortly become Cubists. Perhaps alone of all major Parisian painters of the years around 1907, he did not become involved at this juncture in studying those aspects of Cézanne's art, the structured brush stroke and the abruptly turned or juxtaposed illusionistic plane, which were pointing toward Cubism. Matisse had absorbed these aspects into his own style several years earlier, shortly after he had purchased the **Bathers** from Vollard in 1899, and by 1907 he had no real need to relive that experience.

Thus, Matisse makes no direct contribution to the initial development of Cubism—unless it is possible that Picasso, around 1907, shortly after he had made Matisse's acquaintance through the Steins, was influenced by the sight of such figure studies of 1900 as the **Male Model** (page 57), the pictorial equivalent of the bronze **Slave** (figure 10). These years that witnessed the turbulent evolution of Cubism were, for Matisse, a time of harmony and fulfillment. The trials and contradictions of the previous fifteen years, the era of his debut as a painter, were over. However, simply because he failed to follow the new movement—although he would later

investigate some of its more decorative features, temporarily incorporating them into his art in the years around 1914— it would be a mistake to think of Matisse as slackening off at this point. Rather, his large-scale, simplified decorative style, most in evidence in the figurative work of the period, was his distinctive alternative to Cubism. He was now working alone in a highly personal idiom, in contrast to the Cubists, whose efforts tended to be collaborative or cooperative. A small group of enlightened patrons could be counted on to acquire his major works, and even to propose commissions (as was the case with **Dance** and **Music**). He continued to show his work at the Independent and Autumn Salons, but many of his finest works thereupon vanished into foreign collections (especially those of the Russians Shchukin and Morosov), and were thus not readily available to be seen by younger painters or critics. It would obviously be wrong to assume that Matisse had been absorbed into anything like an establishment coterie at this point. Nevertheless, the avant-garde would henceforth be identified with the Cubists, the Fauve "movement" having, to all intents and purposes, vanished by 1908.

Moreover, Matisse's status as a maître was to a degree established by the opening of an Académie Matisse in 1908, which lasted until 1911, although the artist became progressively less interested in his professorial duties toward the end. This is also the epoch of his lengthy article "Notes of a Painter," published in *La Grande Revue*, December 25, 1908. This article, combining both theoretical and practical reflections, probably grew out of his teaching experience—weekly atelier criticisms, some of which were recorded by Sarah Stein, one of his pupils and a respected friend, whose husband Michael was a patron of the Académie Matisse. Sarah Stein's notes dating from 1908 were published only in 1951 (as Appendix A of Alfred Barr's extensive monograph on the painter), and they form an interesting companion to "Notes

24

25

of a Painter." From all reports, Matisse's teaching might be judged traditional, as he was concerned with providing his many students (few of whom were French) with a firm classical grounding, echoing much of his own experience of fifteen years before. Likewise, "Notes of a Painter" is a classical, though certainly not academic, statement, especially when read in the context of the Cubist, Futurist, and Abstract art manifestoes that appeared over the next decade.

Matisse's observations in this article are remarkably lucid. His theory is actually extracted from his own practice as a painter, and yet these concepts are so all-encompassing as to provide a multitude of applications. After apologizing for addressing his audience in verbal rather than in pictorial form, he states:

What I am after, above all, is expression.... I am unable to distinguish between the feeling I have for life and my way of expressing it.

Expression to my way of thinking does not consist of the passion mirrored upon a human face or betrayed by a violent gesture. The whole arrangement of my pictures is expressive. The place occupied by figures or objects, the empty spaces around them, the proportions, everything plays a part.

These remarks can most immediately be set alongside such contemporary paintings as **Harmony in Red** (actually, as his lines were written, still **Harmony in Blue**) of 1908–9 (page 71). More interesting, however, is the discovery that these fundamental concepts apply to the structure of a powerful Fauve study such as **The Green Stripe** (page 61), which at first glance seems to be impulsive, Expressionistic in countenance, and only later strikes us as rationally expressive as a color composition. Matisse's notion of "expression" is also perfectly reflected in his several versions of **Dance**, where the integral, abstract quality of the line serves to convey the nature of the strenuous action, making possible the progressive reduction and simplification of the figural image as the artist returns over and over again to this theme. Matisse continues:

26 **La Serpentine** 1909
Bronze 22 1/4 in. high
The Museum of Modern Art, New York
Gift of Abby Aldrich Rockefeller

27 **Still Life after De Heem** 1915–17
Oil on canvas, 71 x 87 3/4 in.
Florene M. Schoenborn-Samuel A. Marx Collection, New York

27

26

Composition is the art of arranging in a decorative manner the various elements at the painter's disposal for the expression of his feelings.... All that is not useful in the picture is detrimental. A work of art must be harmonious in its entirety; for superfluous details would, in the mind of the beholder, encroach upon the essential elements.

It is remarkable that this doctrine, hardly more than a rephrasing of classicizing ideals that reach back to the Renaissance, was the conceptual scaffolding upon which Matisse constructed not merely his monumental decorative style of this period but also the more intimate, small-scale manner of the 1920s and the once again decorative, even more architectural style of the late 1940s and early 1950s. These lines, together with those quoted below, could serve as a commentary to such diverse works as the delicate **Still Life with Apples on Pink Cloth** of about 1925 (page 107), or the vast, abstract **The Snail** of 1953 (page 127).

Speaking of the "condensation of sensations which constitutes a picture," Matisse describes his approach to one of his major motifs:

Supposing I want to paint the body of a woman: first of all I endow it with grace and charm, but I know that something more than that is necessary. I try to condense the meaning of this body by drawing its essential lines. The charm will then become less apparent at first glance, but in the long run it will begin to emanate from the new

28 **Sleeping Nude** c. 1916
Oil on canvas, 37 3/8 x 76 3/4 in.
Private collection, New York

28

image. This image at the same time will be enriched by a wider meaning, a more comprehensively human one, while the charm, being less apparent, will not be its only characteristic. It will be merely one element in the general conception of the figure.

There could be no better explanation of the method by which the artist developed the composition of **Le Luxe** from the first to the second version. Often, in subsequent works, we can see a similar process in operation, though occasionally, as in the confrontation of **The Music Lesson** (figure 31) with **The Piano Lesson** (page 101), we cannot be sure that the application of the above-quoted arguments concerning "condensation" will tell us which of the two canvases was conceived and executed first, this because of a relatively abrupt change of style that was occurring in the artist's work at this time, a decade after the writing of "Notes of a Painter." Much later, however, in the painting of the **Pink Nude** (1935), Matisse had the canvas photographed many times in the course of its execution, revealing a process in which the image is distilled and reduced to an increasingly arbitrary arabesque, the inner modeling being correspondingly flattened in the process.

By 1910 Matisse's work was being shown abroad, notably in Germany, Russia, and the United States. In New York City Matisse was introduced via his drawings, selected by Edward Steichen and presented by his fellow photographer Alfred Stieglitz at his "291" Gallery in 1908 and 1910. Remarkably,

two noted specialists in early Italian painting, Bernard Berenson and Frank Jewett Mather, were among the artist's earliest and most articulate champions. Berenson's retort to *The Nation*, apropos of its slighting review of the 1908 Autumn Salon, attacked the ridiculing observations of the magazine's correspondent: "I have the conviction that he [Matisse] has, after twenty years of very earnest searching, at last found the great highroad travelled by all the best masters of the visual arts for the last sixty centuries at least. Indeed, he is singularly like them in every essential respect. He is a magnificent draughtsman and a great designer."

Mather, writing two years later in the New York *Evening Post*, refers to Matisse's concept of the body as a "powerful machine working within certain limits of balance," adding later: "It differs in no essential respect from that of great draughtsmen of all ages. A Matisse drawing, looked at without prejudice, is no more bizarre than a study of action by Hokusai or Michelangelo. It belongs in the great tradition of all art that has envisaged the human form in terms of energy and counterpoise."

Continuing by drawing analogies between these contemporary works and certain recently discovered tempera studies by Tintoretto, Mather notes: "The Frenchman is a kind of modern Pollaiuolo." Given that Mather admits his unfamiliarity with Matisse's paintings, and that in 1910 he would not have known of **Dance**, on which the artist was then working, this is a most prescient comparison. The tense interrelationship of the figures in Pollaiuolo's famed engraving of the

29 **The Studio, Quai Saint-Michel** 1916
Oil on canvas, 57 1/2 x 45 3/4 in.
The Phillips Collection, Washington, D.C.

30 **Mlle. Yvonne Landsberg** 1914
Oil on canvas, 58 x 38 1/2 in.
Philadelphia Museum of Art
The Louise and Walter Arensberg Collection

29

30

Battle of the Nudes possesses many of the qualities of tense action and energy that Matisse introduces in the Shchukin version of **Dance**; in both images the energy is expressed through the abstract flow and abrupt arresting of movement in the lines themselves.

What is especially interesting in the commentaries of both Berenson and Mather is that they establish Matisse's importance in relation to historical figures of commonly accepted worth. Writing in a different cultural context, Apollinaire in 1909 indulged in this paradox: "To tell the truth, M. Henri Matisse is an innovator, but he renovates rather than innovates." Potentially meaningless, this bon mot nonetheless aptly makes an important point concerning the artist's position vis-à-vis the Cubist avant-garde of the day, and also characterizes the artist's philosophy as revealed in "Notes of a Painter." However contemporary and unsettling Matisse's paintings may have been to many at the time—in terms of bold patterning, simplifications of volume, and interplay of color—his roots in the past were at least implic-

itly present; in fact, he made his attitude unmistakable in a passage from the "Notes": "I feel very strongly the bond between my old works and my recent ones. But I do not think the way I thought yesterday. My fundamental thoughts have not changed but have evolved and my modes of expression have followed my thoughts. I do not repudiate any of my paintings but I would not paint one of them in the same way had I to do it again."

For an artist whose destiny was to reach so far beyond the confining limits of that nineteenth-century realism in which he started, it is remarkable that he did not feel the need to disown his earlier work. Instead, it remained important to him, and he could carry the weight of his accumulated personal history with grace and indulgence. The ultimately transcendental nature of his late work, if not as obvious as in a Kandinsky or a Mondrian, was nonetheless recognized by Matisse himself in 1953, in a brief introduction to a publication on his chapel at Vence (page 123). There he noted how the Beaux-Arts teachers of his youth had valued only those observations made after nature, and derided anything coming from the imagination as mere "chiqué." He continues: "Throughout my career I have reacted against this opinion, to which I could not submit myself, and this struggle has been the source of the different avatars along my way, during which I have sought for possibilities of expression beyond the literal copy."

Without doubt, the tension between the subject as perceived and the demands of his artistic materials and means provided a permanent source for renewal in Matisse's art.

For many observers, **Dance** and **Music** remain the climactic works of the artist. Commissioned in 1909, painted and exhibited at the Autumn Salon in 1910, temporarily rejected but finally accepted by Shchukin, they represent, in effect, two-thirds of a vision for the expressive decoration of an artist's studio, the final third of which is represented by **Five Bathers** (**Composition II**; figure 21), a small study of about 1910 which is almost certainly the first project for **Bathers by the River** (page 97). While the completed monumental version of Matisse's **Bathers** (1917) is one of his most important ventures in the direction of a decorative Cubism, the early study is in a manner consonant with **Dance** and **Music**, and evokes the ambiance and, in a more generalized way, the theme of **Le Luxe** (1907). **Five Bathers** also evokes certain compositions of Gauguin in both theme and layout. Matisse was familiar with Gauguin's work as early as the late 1890s, and the importance of his influence in the development of the younger artist's larger figurative compositions, not to mention his choice of motifs, has yet to be fully explored.

Because of the overwhelming clarity of composition in these pictures and the way in which they sum up and partly conclude ideas launched earlier in the decade, they have tended to obscure the importance of the next major series of large-scale works, the four so-called "Symphonic Interiors" (pages 77–83), all works of 1911. In fact, the major paintings of these two productive years, 1910 and 1911, would seem to be intimately linked as different aspects of the studio theme. **Dance**, **Music**, and **Bathers** each addresses itself to the question of decorating the artist's studio; three of the four "Symphonic Interiors"—**Red Studio**, **Pink Studio**, and **Still Life with Aubergines**—are concerned with a spiritualized, decorative "representation" of it; the fourth, **The Painter's Family**, establishes a domestic contact and context for them. When these seven monumental works are considered together, we discover a fascinating dialogue between the various layers of art and life. We are simultaneously aware of the life of the model or motif and the complementary life of the design or composition, and especially the interplay between the two. Together they represent a manifesto on the creative process that is more fundamental and original than

31

the concise passages of "Notes of a Painter." It would not seem that the four major paintings of 1911 were conceived as a series, given their varying dimensions. More likely they multiplied in an entirely spontaneous fashion and set the stage for later, though less monumental, pictorial views into the artist's studio. The chief difference in the later pictures is the frequent inclusion, within the image itself, of the artist's own presence.

Of the smaller paintings of 1911, **Blue Window** (figure 24) is perhaps the most remarkable. Though unrelated in format, it follows the coloristic and compositional principles of **Red Studio**. That is to say, the entire ground of the picture is of a single hue, although individual objects are allowed to retain their own local color. This results in an effect in which the objects seem to float in a kind of aqueous space, an imaginary pictorial atmosphere analogous to the aquariums to be found in the numerous paintings of goldfish of this period. **Blue Window** was painted for the famous couturier and bon vivant Paul Poiret, who refused to accept it. Given Poiret's later patronage of the designers of Art Deco in the 1920s, together with the subject of the painting, an open window, one is inclined to suspect that the present picture might originally have been destined to serve as part of a coordinated interior design by one of the fashionable decorators of the post-Art Nouveau epoch. The style that Matisse developed, or,

32A-C **Three Sisters** 1916–17
  Triptych, oil on canvas, each panel 77 x 38
  © The Barnes Foundation, Merion, Pennsylvania

32A   B   C

more exactly, "condensed" here, one based upon comparing a variety of spherical and rounded forms, is one of his more abstract, and would certainly lend itself to architectural purposes.

After the protracted effort of the previous five years, with much of it related to two intertwined themes—the revived arcadian composition and the heroically scaled interior, both of which were hinged upon Matisse's deep-felt emotions and associations with the studio—it is not surprising that he sought new stimuli to sustain at least a part of his work in the second decade of the century. In 1910 he had traveled to Munich to see an exhibition of Muslim art, in company with his old friend of student days Albert Marquet. Late the following year he returned to North Africa (having been there in 1906), and this trip was followed by another during the winter of 1912–13. His companions on these trips were his Fauve friends Marquet and Charles Camoin. These voyages abroad are unique in his career in that they were working trips, resulting in major series of paintings as well as retained impressions that would serve as the inspiration for

other compositions carried out in the studio after his return. **Park in Tangier** (figure 25) and **Moroccan Garden** (page 85) are representative of the earlier trip, **Zorah on the Terrace** and **Entrance to the Kasbah** (pages 87 and 89) of the second. These remarkably hued, atmospherically intense studies made on the scene hardly prepare us for the synthetic, even symbolic masterpiece **The Moroccans** (page 99). Here, in an unusual tripartite format, the artist, profiting from his essays in a Cubist manner starting in 1914, interjects an effective discontinuity in the visual image. He ruptures the nominal linkage among the three parts of the picture, each of which is held in suspense by black, spatially indeterminate areas, and then reestablishes the picture's unity through the geometric echoing of circular and curved forms among the architecture, the fruits and leaves, and the group of praying figures.

This fragmenting of a single decorative surface into three parts in **The Moroccans** is a device which represents Matisse's belated and partial assimilation of Cubist concepts during the years 1914–17. While a number of significant pictures of this period show hardly a trace of this preoccupation, others represent a very direct effort to come to grips with a style

33 **Moorish Screen** 1922
Oil on canvas, 36 1/4 x 29 in.
Philadelphia Museum of Art
Lisa Norris Elkins Collection

34 **Odalisque with Tambourine** 1926
Oil on canvas, 28 x 21 in.
Collection Mr. and Mrs. William S. Paley, New York

33

34

that in its early phase, around 1907, was inimical to the organic growth of his personal manner. But by 1914 the heroic days of Cubism were over, and its style (termed Synthetic in its later stage) was tending toward decorative flattening and simplification. Moreover, some Cubists were introducing strong colors into their studies of fractured planes and dislocated volumes, in sharp contrast to the more monochromatic tendencies of earlier Cubism. All these developments, seen best perhaps in the works of Juan Gris of around 1914, were leading to a flattened, patterned pictorial surface of vivid, sometimes clashing hues. This development provided a logical opportunity for Matisse to experiment with Cubist devices without breaking with his own idiom. The historical connection was provided by the fact that Matisse and Gris summered together at Collioure in 1914, holding many conversations and, according to Gris, even heated arguments over painting.

 Perhaps not enough has been made of this encounter by students of Matisse's work. However, the major works immediately following 1914, together with many of the minor, would be tinged with Cubist devices, culminating in the

completion of **Bathers by the River** (page 97) in a manner even more architectonic than the originally contemplated layout of 1910. This period, which roughly coincides with the years of World War I, forms a partial rupture with the lyrical and harmonious era centered upon the efforts of 1910–11. It is as if Matisse almost deliberately introduced difficulties into his established style, one that had been enriched by the travels to North Africa of 1911–13, by introducing abrupt paradoxes and even contradictions into his compositions.

 As if to indicate his perplexity and his need to reconsider many basic questions concerning the creative process that he had expounded in the 1908 "Notes of a Painter," he resorted to a device of his pre–1900 student years. In 1893–95 he had made a rather ordinary, if loose, copy of Jan de Heem's **The Dessert** as one of several studies after old masters in the Louvre he did under the tutelage of Gustave Moreau. Interestingly, this would be the title and subject but not the actual source of Matisse's **Desserte** (figure 7) and **Harmony in Red** (page 71). In the years 1915–17 he reworked De Heem's image in a canvas of much larger format, employing an almost pedantically Cubist manner (figure 27). As a

35

36

Cubist reordering of reality, the final result is not especially consistent or profound, and we must conclude that this picture was, for the artist, a testing ground for the discovery of those elements in Cubism that might be harmoniously combined in his own work. As noted elsewhere, **Bathers by the River** still exhibits traces of work done much earlier in a different mode, yet it is the later, Cubist-inclined overpainting that dominates. However, **The Piano Lesson** (page 101), with its massing of flat planes outlined by a grid of horizontal, vertical, and diagonal lines, is perhaps Matisse's most consistent assimilation of the Cubist legacy, a picture that is indebted to that movement and is not merely a collection of incompletely borrowed or reinterpreted devices (as had been the case with the Neo-Impressionist **Luxe, calme et volupté** of 1904, as well as with several of the painter's more superficially Cubistic canvases). Ironically, during or shortly after the execution of **The Piano Lesson** he painted its pendant, **The Music Lesson**, in a ripe, softened style, one which nonetheless makes use of the same basic palette of pinks, greens, and grays, as if to say that having conquered the Cubist question, he could turn his back on it. Yet Cubism did have a

durable effect on his art later—on the large murals of **Dance** (figure 44, page 117) as well as on his late *papiers-découpés*.

The decade subsequent to the Cubist adventure was outwardly one of retrenchment for Matisse. Not only did he abandon for a considerable period the architecturally scaled, geometric structure of such achievements as **The Piano Lesson**, but he abandoned work in large format altogether. Moreover, the coloristic daring of **Red Studio** (1911) and the legendary, mythic scope of **Joy of Life** (1906) are missing from the calm decade of the 1920s, when the artist concerned himself largely with small, Intimist canvases of interiors. These almost invariably reveal improvised studios in hotel rooms or temporary apartments in Nice, which, from 1916 onward, became increasingly the artist's most important working address. Still life and muted landscape also abound during this period, but the interior, normally including the female figure—singly, in pairs, or in trios—is surely the dominant motif. In effect it is a re-creation of the studio theme, now integrated with and enriched by other concepts: the artist's living environment—presented earlier as a single

37 **Nude in the Studio** 1935
Ink, 17 3/4 x 22 3/8 in.
Private collection

37

theme in **The Painter's Family** (page 81)—together with the North African motif—exemplified by the frequent inclusion of costumed or partly costumed odalisques. This dovetailing of earlier motifs into single images is paradoxically accomplished in paintings of rather small scale, in muted if often complex color harmonies, and with soft, pliant contours replacing the taut, astringent design of his earlier work.

Because of this softened style, many commentators have concluded that Matisse had now given up the quest for a contemporary art in which he had been engaged for two decades, and was resting on his laurels. Or, at best, this period is seen as a détente, an entr'acte between Matisse's early and late heroic phases. However, this seemingly undemanding manner contains many pictorial subtleties that would not have been possible on a larger scale; furthermore, it presents the artist's favorite motifs in a new synthesis,

which, on closer examination, is nothing less than the domestication of **Luxe, calme et volupté**. One of the most sumptuous of these paintings is **Moorish Screen** (figure 33). The vantage point is high, helping to create a tension between the plane of the carpeted floor and that of the wall, whose major ornament is the screen of the title. Almost lost in this sumptuous yet delicately colored and lightly-brushed interior are two young women, casually posed in simple white dresses. A mood of indolence is conveyed by this contrast, which in theory ought to be quite abrupt but in fact does not clash at all. Similar unities are to be found in the many and infinitely varied odalisques of the 1920s, in which the play of flesh and fabric is invariably challenging, frequently emphasizing the mutual softness of both, but with the flesh as a more potent reflector of other lights and other colors. Alternatively, as with the **Odalisque with Tambourine**

38 **Nude in the Studio** 1937
Pen, 20 x 15 in.
Indiana University Art Museum, Bloomington

39 **Dancer Resting in Armchair (study for La France)** 1939
Charcoal, 24 3/4 x 18 1/2 in.
Centre Pompidou, Paris

38

39

(figure 34), the artist becomes impatient with these soft, reflective tones and indulges in a more stringent interplay of painted surfaces, especially between the figure and its surroundings. The most striking of these souvenirs of North Africa painted in Nice is **Decorative Figure** (page 111), which conveys the paradox of soft texture and a light almost totally absorbed by the nap of the carpets and hangings, contrasted with a strength and clarity of design represented by the forcefully modeled figure and the inventive variations of the flat fabric patterns.

The studio nude, or odalisque, is a motif closely associated with the period of the 1920s, but it should not be forgotten that this normally recumbent figure is a theme that recurs both early and late. **Blue Nude** (1907; figure 13) has already been mentioned, together with her much later sister, the rather Ingresque **Pink Nude** (1935). Larger in dimensions than either of these important works—in fact, lifesize— is the little-known **Sleeping Nude** (c. 1916; figure 28), which is shown being painted in **Studio, Quai Saint-Michel**, of the same year (figure 29). In some of the paintings of the 1920s the artist's presence is clearly indicated, either by the inclusion of his figure or a fragment thereof, or through the device

of the mirror reflection (the mirror being, like the open window, an analogy with the frame and contents of the created picture). One major realization of this motif is in the extensive series of pen-and-ink drawings **Nude in the Studio** (figures 37, 38) which dominate the period 1935–37. These offer seemingly infinite variations on the nude model, her mirror reflection together with that, frequently, of the artist, whose hand or figure fragment is even occasionally present in the foreground of the sheet. This dialogue between the artist and his model becomes increasingly important in the later mutations of the studio motif, although it had been announced as early as 1903 in **Carmelina** (page 57).

He was occupied throughout the 1920s with the paintings of reconstructed harems along with their passive, accommo-dating occupants, so comparison with Delacroix, and even more significantly with Ingres, is inescapable. Ingres was, as is well known, rediscovered and newly appreciated by artists of the Cubist generation, and Picasso, as early as 1915, was executing drawings that would seem to be specific references to the style and presentation of the great French Neoclassicist. It cannot be proved that Matisse was aware of Ingres's

40 **Lady in Blue** 1937
   Oil on canvas, 36 1/2 x 29 in.
   Collection Mrs. John Wintersteen, Philadelphia

41 J.-A.-D. Ingres: **Mme. Inès Moitessier Seated** 1856
   Oil on canvas, 47 1/4 x 36 1/4 in.
   The National Gallery, London

40

41

Golden Age at the time of **Joy of Life** or shortly thereafter, but nonetheless there are significant parallels in their work that point to a more serious concern with Ingres on Matisse's part from the late 1920s onward. The Neoclassic component in Matisse's art is, for the most part, subterranean and complex. His work of 1900–10 is an expansion and refinement of Cézanne's treatment of a favorite classical theme, namely the **Bather**, largely purged of its specific mythological element. In 1918 he met Renoir, and certainly something of the delicate sensuous touch of Matisse's paintings of the 1920s is indebted to this contact. Renoir's late classicism was lacking in the strong arabesque characteristic of Matisse's work of this mid-period, but toward the end of the 1920s a concern for linear structure reappears, and this seems coincident with a serious study of Ingres more than a decade after Picasso had followed a similar path. This was not a capricious turn in Matisse's development, any more than was his interest in certain stylized aspects of Cubism around 1914–17. Rather, it responded to an inner, organic need in his continual growth as an artist.

The Ingresque aspect of the **Pink Nude** (figure 14) has already been mentioned, but the portrait **Woman with a Veil**

(page 115) indicates a much earlier beginning for this preoccupation. The frontal pose, with the chin resting on the cupped hand, the forearm balanced on the knee, is especially typical of the works of the earlier master. Even more striking is the resemblance in pose between **Lady in Blue** (figure 40) and Ingres's portrait of **Mme. Moitessier** (figure 41), where the pose has been reversed and the recumbent hand is holding a string of beads in place of the folded fan. Matisse, of course, maintains a greater simplicity and symmetry of outline, and is even more drastic in his avoidance of interior modeling of the figure. Just as the final results achieved by these respective masters of the nineteenth and twentieth centuries are suggestively parallel, the means by which they achieved their uniquely concentrated images is similar. Both began with relatively informal, naturally posed studies (Matisse's early versions of **Lady in Blue** were on the canvas itself; they were photographed before being rubbed out or painted over), and from there proceeded to the contrived, hieratic images of the definitive versions. The procedure adopted by Matisse in this and in similar works like **Pink Nude** or **Music** (page 121) is not simply the grafting of Ingres's habitual compositional practice onto his own work.

42A-E **Preparatory studies for Dance** 1930–31
Pencil, dimensions varied
Musée Matisse, Nice-Cimiez

43 **Dance I** 1931–32
Oil on canvas, 140 1/2 x 42 ft. 1 in.
Musée d'Art Moderne de la Ville de Paris

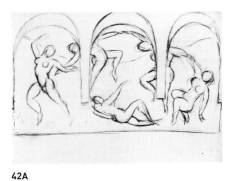

42A

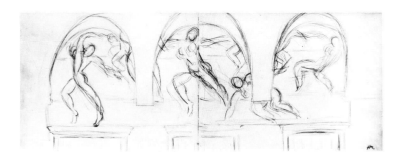

B

C

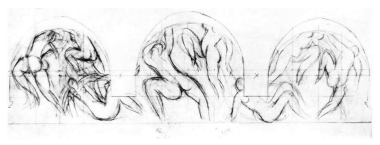

D

E

43

44

Instead, it is the perfection and refinement of his doctrine as presented in "Notes of a Painter" more than a quarter century before. That he could almost coincidentally arrive at a somewhat Ingresque phase in the 1930s is but one more indication of the traditionalistic orientation of his ideals and the thoroughness of his familiarity with the works of earlier masters.

Matisse's art had from time to time, beginning about 1910, shown evidence of leaping the bounds of conventional framed pictures into the area of architectural decoration. This literally took place with the two full-scale versions of **Dance** (figures 43 and 44), which, together with the numerous preparatory studies (figure 42, page 117), are among Matisse's most ambitious. In fact, it was not a new project but the development and adaptation, to a different and arbitrary format, of the dance theme which had begun, possibly as an adaptation from Ingres or Signac, in the center distance of the **Joy of Life** twenty-five years earlier. The numerous pencil studies leading up to the two final versions show the gradual mutation of the old theme, the ring of dancers being broken by physical exhaustion and as a consequence of the tripartite arched space into which the mural had to fit (under the vaults of the central hall in the Barnes Foundation, Merion, Pennsylvania). That we are so fortunate as to possess two full-scale versions of this distinctive architectural composition is due to the accident of the artist having received erroneous dimensions in the first instance, and his stubbornness in starting over again with still another variation when this fact became clear. The early pencil sketches as well as the color studies show figures scaled to the contours of the arches, but these figures grow progressively in size until they become enormous, suggestive fragments that overrun the scale of the architecture. Indeed, it is in scale rather than color that Matisse forces the effect of the Barnes **Dance** and of its mismeasured predecessor. Many commentators have regretted the pale pinks, blues, and grays of these murals, feeling them to be a step down from a previous intensity of expression, but in fact the restrained hues were

deliberately designed to blend with the restrained Neoclassic architecture and to avoid competition with other paintings (by Seurat and Cézanne as well as Matisse) that were hung on the lower walls of the same vaulted gallery. Moreover, by grandly enlarging the scale of the figures, the possibilities of decorative flatness in the entire composition were enhanced.

Matisse's own view of the final results in the two monumental completed versions, both of which differ in significant ways from these intermediate studies, is revealing of his aims: "The Merion panel was made especially for the place. Isolated, I don't consider it as anything more than a fragment of architecture." Considering that much later, in the chapel at Vence (1948–51), Matisse was able to carry out an entire architectural ensemble, this attitude is especially important.

Rarely has a twentieth-century artist been offered the opportunity to work at this monumental scale; paradoxically, in the months during which Matisse was at work on the Barnes commission, he was engaged by the publisher Albert Skira to illustrate a deluxe edition of a selection of poems by Mallarmé. Nothing could have been further removed in size than a project of this genre (it was, in fact, Matisse's first venture into the art of the illustrated book), and yet there is an astonishing resemblance between his efforts for each project. Both were the subject of minute study in a multitude of preparatory drawings, though in the case of **Dance** the final result was a vast mural painting, while in the case of the Mallarmé it was a publication featuring twenty-nine full-page etchings. Although the format of the book is not out of the ordinary for luxurious limited editions of this sort (9 3/4 by 13 inches), the illustrated pages possess something of the monumentality of the contemporary murals. Matisse chose to design his plates to equal the full size of the page, dispensing with conventional margins, and to reduce the incidental details of the preparatory sketches to the point where only an etched line of remarkably even weight was used to suggest volume or surrounding space. Consequently, both mural and etched page represent, each according to the nature of its

45 **Nymph in the Forest** 1936
Oil on canvas, 96 x 78 in.
Collection Jean Matisse, Paris

45

proper material and function, the ultimate condensation of his perception or concept of a given motif. Both seem rendered without effort, with the ease and fluency of experience, and yet both were prepared with minute and painstaking care. Other illustrated books would follow in the two decades and more of life remaining to Matisse, but if he might, in his Ronsard or in *Jazz*, equal or surpass the originality of concept, he would never duplicate the ethereal refinement or spacious contours of the 1932 Mallarmé.

Now in his sixties, Matisse did not slacken his efforts in the wake of the completion of the Barnes mural in 1933. His efforts continued in several mediums. In 1935 he was commissioned to do a series of etchings for Joyce's *Ulysses*, and instead of illustrating the modern story, he returned to the antique legend to find his subjects for the six plates. In 1935–36 he executed the tapestry cartoon **Window in Tahiti** (page 119), and in the latter year painted the equally monumental **Nymph in the Forest** (figure 45), which was also probably intended to become a tapestry. Here, reverting to the Nymph and Satyr theme, he develops the figure of the recumbent nymph from the fallen figure in the center lunette of the Barnes **Dance**. A monumental drawing of the figures alone, more than five feet in height, was done at this time, but

in the early 1940s Matisse drastically revised and simplified it. The subject had been employed for one of the Mallarmé etchings as well, indicating once more the artist's continual reworking of both subjects and poses in a variety of mediums, as well as a variety of scales. Finally, in 1937, he was asked to do a design for Massine's ballet *Rouge et Noir*. For this project he returned, appropriately enough, to the composition of the Barnes murals, employing that particular architectural form, together with his abstract background, as the basis for the backdrop (the dancing figures being understandably absent from this design, as real dancers would be performing in front of it). And, continuing in an architectural vein, in 1938 Matisse also painted an overmantel decoration for the Nelson Rockefeller apartment in New York. The painting of four female figures, sitting, reading, and sleeping, quite overwhelms the modest dimensions of the fireplace proper. The painting is over nine feet in height, and is framed by an unusual meandering contour that evokes memories of the Art Nouveau movement which had flourished at the time of the artist's youth.

Of the easel paintings of the period, two of the most splendid are **The Conservatory** (figure 46) and **The Dream** (**Sleeping Woman**; figure 48). **The Conservatory** develops a theme frequently encountered in the Intimist works of the 1920s but now monumentalized and simplified, even though the picture's actual dimensions are relatively modest. As with the two figures in the 1939 **Music** (page 75), the problem was one of establishing either a contrapuntal or a parallel pose for the two women: here he opted for the former, while in **Music** he chose a parallel pose, with the two figures echoing each other. In **The Conservatory**, the patterns of the two bodies share their importance with the five heart-shaped leaves that provide a virtually heraldic background motif. As for **The Dream**, it is one of the artist's most remarkable compositions based on the single figure. The subject grows out of an earlier painting (1935) of the head and shoulders of a sleeping model. Now, however, the motif is treated within a boldly fused, all-encompassing circular snail-like motif. One is immediately impelled to see here a variation on a theme dear to Picasso in the late 1920s and early 1930s. Indeed, this is only one example (and a rather late one at that) of exchanges of motif or pose between the two painters. Moreover, **The Dream** would seem to be the ultimate outcome of his preoccupation over the past decade with an arbitrary, Ingresque type of arabesque. Just before executing **The Dream**, Matisse painted a bright figure in red and yellow, **La France** (figure 49), in which the heart-shaped leaves of **The Conservatory** are transformed into the figure itself. Even more remarkable are the two nearly identical drawings (figure 39) that served as studies for this painting, which seems to have been

46 The Conservatory 1938
Oil on canvas, 29 x 23⅞ in.
Collection Joseph Pulitzer, Jr., St. Louis

47 The Dream 1935
Oil on canvas, 31⅞ x 25⅝ in.
Private collection, New York

48 The Dream (Sleeping Woman) 1940
Oil on canvas, 31⅞ x 25½ in.
Collection M. and Mme Georges Duthuit, Paris

49 La France 1939
Oil on canvas, 18⅛ x 15 in.
Contemporary Art Establishment, Zurich

46

48

47

49

50 **Dancer and Armchair, Black Background** 1942
Oil on canvas, 19 3/4 x 25 5/8 in.
Collection Mrs. Marcel Duchamp, New York

51 **Asia** 1946
Oil on canvas, 45 3/4 x 32 in.
Collection Mrs. Mollie Parnis Livingston, New York

50

51

carried out in a burst of patriotic enthusiasm during the months immediately following the declaration of war on September 3, 1939.

Matisse at first considered leaving France after the defeat in June 1940, but changed his mind and left Paris for Bordeaux, finally finding his way back to Nice. Once again, as in 1914–18, the artist's career was partly overshadowed by hostilities. By the fall of 1940 he was having difficulty even in finding colors and canvases. More serious was the onset of an intestinal ailment which necessitated two successive operations in March 1941, and very nearly proved fatal. From this point on, Matisse was bedridden for many hours of the day, but this physical discomfiture did not slacken his enthusiasm and ability for new work. It is interesting to note that the artist began his professional career in the wake of a slow recovery from an appendicitis operation during his twenty-first year, 1890. A little more than a half century later a similar if more drastic ailment marked the beginning of the last and, for many, the most glorious phase of his career.

Matisse's last paintings, such as **Dancer and Armchair, Black Background** (figure 50), **Asia** (figure 51), and **Interior with Black Fern** (figure 52), all develop themes that he had been working on in the 1930s or even earlier. One of his very last paintings on canvas, **Interior with Egyptian Curtain** (figure 53) the artist virtually abandoned this medium in 1948—returns to the theme of the open window, carrying us back nearly a half century in his work but with echoes of the interiors of the 1920s. The right margin of the picture is dominated by a curtain of black, with red, green, yellow, and white ornamentation. Beyond the dish of fruit one's view through the window is completely dominated by the foliage of a palm tree whose curving branches are made to intersect with the

rectangular divisions of the window. This landscape fragment is painted in bright blues, greens, and yellows, with accents of black throughout serving to bind together the spaces of the interior and exterior.

Contemporary with these late paintings are some of the artist's most remarkable drawings. An important sequence of these, *Dessins: thèmes et variations*, with a preface by Louis Aragon, was sumptuously published in the midst of the Occupation, in 1943. During this decade Matisse also designed eight luxurious limited editions of various authors, ranging from Ronsard and Charles d'Orléans to Baudelaire and Montherlant. The most remarkable of these volumes is *Jazz* (1947), a portfolio of twenty colorplates printed in pochoir after a series of *papiers-découpés* that date as early as 1943. The plates for *Jazz* were not composed to a text, but rather Matisse composed a text of meditations on his art to accompany the vivid images. The majority of these are drawn from the theme of the circus, a subject that the artist had never before touched (though of course it figures in a major way in the early works of Picasso). Supplementing the circus

52

53

themes are a single classical subject, The Fall of Icarus; ornamental landscapes, one titled *The Lagoon*; and, finally, two mysterious subjects, *The Toboggan* and *Destiny*. In the informal, conversational text he speaks of "drawing with scissors," adding: "To cut to the quick in color reminds me of direct cutting in sculpture. This book has been conceived in that spirit."

Matisse's method of *papier-découpé* is rather different from the collage technique exploited by the Cubists and Dadaists several decades earlier. His procedure was to cover sheets of paper with a uniform color in gouache; then, with one or several colors at hand, he would proceed to cut out the forms and paste them (or have them pasted) on the picture's surface. He had first made use of this technique, though only for purposes of trying out certain hues, while painting the Barnes versions of **Dance** in 1931–33. However, from 1948 until his death in 1954 this would be Matisse's preferred medium. While the illustrations for *Jazz* were, naturally, of rather small format, Matisse quickly realized the possibilities for employing *papier-découpé* on a grandiose

scale—a discovery that led to the great monumental works of the last five years of his life.

The **Dominican Chapel of the Rosary, Vence** (page 123) occupied much of his time during 1948–51. As an artist he successively and simultaneously mastered the arts of painting, drawing, and sculpture, as well as the making of prints in various mediums; there is every reason to think that with sympathetic technical and professional collaboration Matisse could have reached equal heights in architectural design, especially in the realm of creating total interiors.

Working with architectural models and with *papier-découpé* studies for windows as well as for the priests' chasubles, drawing at large scale for the painted and glazed tiles, and modeling in clay for the bronze altar crucifix must have taxed Matisse's strength. However, upon the chapel's completion he set to work on the surprisingly large number of designs that he was yet to accomplish in *papier-découpé*. Some of these projects are largely decorative or architectural in purpose, vast ornamental schemes, certain of which were subsequently executed in glazed tile. Others were for

54 **Blue Nude IV** 1952
Papier-découpé, 40 1/2 x 29 1/8 in.
Private collection, Paris

54

55 **Acrobats** 1952
Gouache and *papier-découpé*, 102 x 96 in.
Collection Sheldon Solow, New York

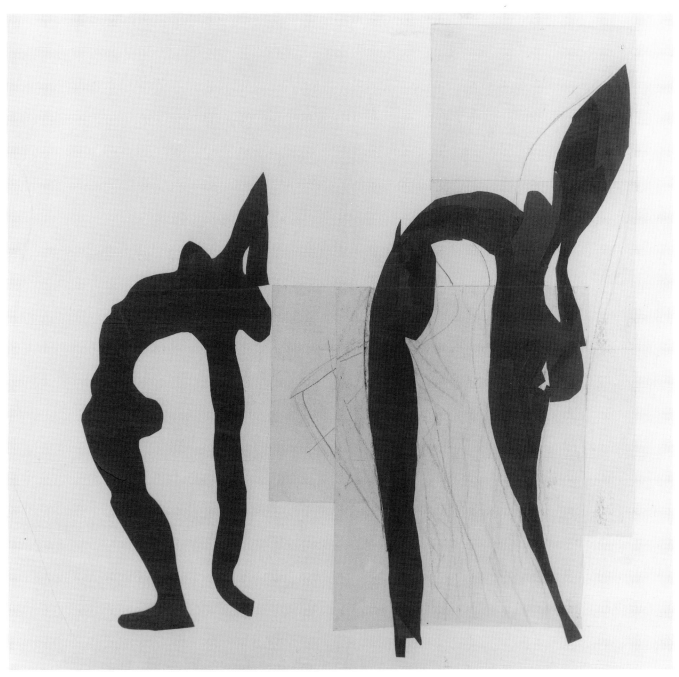

55

stained-glass windows, and still others were figure studies or thematic compositions—as, for example, **The Sorrows of the King** (page 125). Many of these were pinned to the wall of his studio and other rooms of his apartment in Nice, thus becoming a living, constantly changing and growing series of decorations, an expanded and modified realization of the program that he had described to Estienne in 1909 for the decoration of an artist's studio.

Among the most austere of the *papiers-découpés* are the series of seated **Blue Nudes** (figure 54). The pose should be compared to the 1925 **Decorative Figure** (page 111) and may also be related to Picasso's bonelike **Seated Bather** (1930), while the flattened, stylized rendering represents still another step toward the ornamental, beyond the degree found in **Pink Nude** (1935). Significantly, Matisse wished that these late works be reproduced without any indications of the slight variations in color intensity, and without the pencil marks on the white paper behind. Hence the present reproduction violates the artist's wishes, but serves to indicate the painstaking, deliberate care that he took to achieve the effect

56

57

of spontaneity. In fact, the improvised quality of so much of his late work was arrived at only after much consideration and reflection, and only rarely does accident serve to control the final product. **The Acrobats** (figure 55) are over-lifesize figures that, in their elastic posturing, seem to grow out of the later versions of **Dance**, while their subject is reminiscent of the circus theme that runs through Jazz. The most ambitious of the figurative *papiers-découpés* of this year is **The Swimming Pool** (figure 63), fifty-four feet in total length (only half is shown in the reproduction). Here the blue figures are once again set against a white ground, but this time their leapings and cavortings carry them well beyond the upper and even the lower margins of the paper. The ambitions that had been fired two decades earlier while working on the **Dance** murals had not

been quieted by age or physical infirmity. Here the figures are distorted in a way that must have been suggested by the appearance of objects seen through a surface of water: it is not clear whether we are looking down into the pool or are viewing it in imaginary cross section. In fact, some of the figures seem to be leaping, dolphin-like, from the surface upward, others seem to be diving into the water from above, and still others seem to be merely floating passively on its surface. There is nothing quite like this near-abstract concentration of fluent energy in his previous figurative works save for the various versions of **Dance**, and the inescapable conclusion is that with **The Swimming Pool** we are being treated to a water ballet.

Inexhaustibly, Matisse created several more or less

58 **Back III** Probably 1916–17
Bronze, 74 1/2 x 44 x 6 in.

59 **Back IV** 1930
Bronze, 74 x 44 1/4 x 6 in.
The Museum of Modern Art, New York
Mrs. Simon Guggenheim Fund

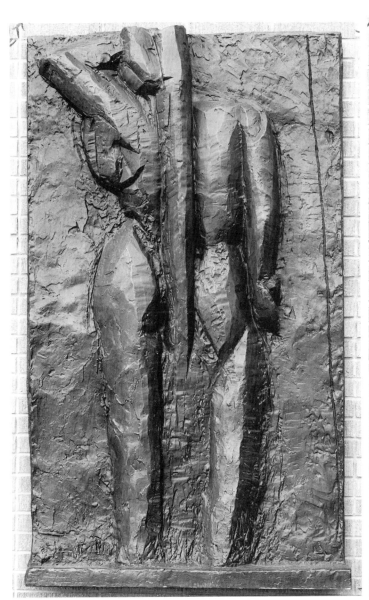

58

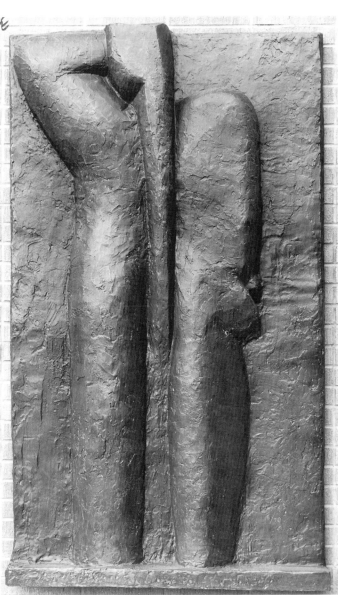

59

"conventional" pictures in *papier-découpé* at this juncture, notably **The Sorrows of the King** (page 125) and **The Snail** (page 127). Beyond these, several photographs (figures 60–62) of the artist's studio, taken in 1953, show us many of the works of the last full year of his life. The very nature of the photographs themselves calls up the painted images of the artist's studio which he had so often created over the years, though less frequently after the late 1920s. Here we see small, intimate studies side by side with immense decorative schemes that overwhelm the relatively modest space of the studio. It would almost seem as if the artist had "directed" the photographer in his work, and that only through this medium can we completely grasp the special personal meaning and sense of fulfillment these works had for Matisse.

Matisse's final legacy is thus extremely personal, the inward realization of concepts that were in his mind for much of his working life. With the most abstract and ornamental of the *papiers-découpés* he had to a degree separated himself from the other surviving members of the École de Paris (Picasso, Braque, Dufy, Derain, Chagall, to mention only the older generation). This break would, however, insure him a special place among the heroes of much younger artists. American painters of various ages and tendencies have been attracted to Matisse's work, especially since he seemed to offer an antidote to the all-pervasive influence of Cubism. Artists like Ellsworth Kelly and Frank Stella were inspired by him at different points in their careers, and Pop artist Tom Wesselman has directly copied paintings by Matisse as

60 Matisse in his studio, 1953

61 A corner of the studio, 1953

62 A wall in the studio, 1953

63 **The Swimming Pool** 1952
   Project for a ceramic mural, gouache and *papier-découpé* on canvas
   Half reproduced, size of whole 8 ft. 4 1/2 in. x 54 ft.
   Collection M. and Mme. Georges Duthuit, Paris

60

61

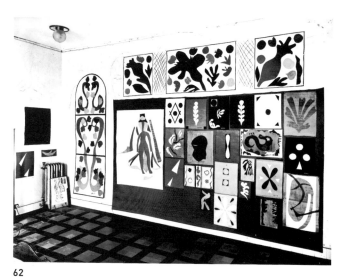

62

63

accessories in his own compositions. Roy Lichtenstein, after having previously adapted images from Picasso and Mondrian, based the iconography of his still-life and studio paintings of 1973 on the French master's handling of these themes. Published and widely exhibited in the early 1960s, Matisse's final creations served to stimulate the efforts and goals of a new generation of late twentieth-century artists. Indeed, he was concerned with them and their fate almost to the very end. Writing in 1948 to Henry Clifford (who was then organizing an exhibition of his work at the Philadelphia Museum of Art), he observed: "I have always tried to hide my own efforts and wished my works to have the lightness and joyousness of a springtime which never lets anyone suspect the labors it has cost. So I am afraid that the young, seeing in my work only that apparent facility and negligence in the drawing, will use this as an excuse for dispensing with certain efforts which I believe necessary."

The student of Matisse's work thus has a twofold task: he must maintain a freshness of vision so that the purity and succinctness of the completed picture is properly conveyed and at the same time he must remember that the effects of spontaneity ever present in the artist's mature works were achieved only through severe self-criticism, patient reflection, and persistent revision.

plates

Painted c. 1894
Oil on canvas, 24 1/4 x 18 7/8 in.
Musée National d'Art Moderne, Paris

Woman Reading (La Liseuse)

Matisse achieved his first public success (prematurely, as it turned out) when this modest, intimate interior was exhibited in 1896 at the Salon du Champ-de-Mars, an independent but not radical rival of the official Salon, organized by the Société Nationale des Beaux-Arts and presided over by Puvis de Chavannes. Although he was still nominally a student in Moreau's atelier, the success of this work, and three others that accompanied it, merited him an associate membership in the Société Nationale that year. It was purchased by the state, and, having been admired by the family of President Félix Faure, it was hung in the apartments of their summer residence at the Château de Rambouillet. It was installed in the Musée National d'Art Moderne only after World War II.

Although Matisse at the time was not yet in complete command of the technical resources of painting, as would become clear in later, more ambitious yet rather laborious works like **La Desserte** (figure 7), he was already quite capable of realizing a modest effort such as this. Based indirectly upon his appreciation of Chardin and of the Dutch paintings that he would have seen in the museum at Lille before coming to Paris as an art student in 1892, it also suggests his study of Corot. The theme is furthermore prophetic: the subject of a woman reading recurs in his paintings as late as the 1940s, and the interior itself, almost studio-like with its emphasis upon pictures on the wall (unfortunately not identifiable, as would be the case later), is suggestive of a major preoccupation throughout the artist's oeuvre.

At the time of its painting Matisse had little or no knowledge of contemporary trends, and this interior is largely the result of museum study; while it was a reflection of the work that he was doing in Moreau's studio (see, for example, **Studio of Gustave Moreau**, figure 6), it owes nothing to his master's manner or subjects. Though occasionally passed over as an imitative or conservative work, it is remarkably independent of any one predominant influence. Even its Intimist qualities, which might suggest an influence from the Nabi quarter and specifically from the work of Vuillard, are misleading, as that painter's work of this epoch was much more schematic and flattened than is the case here, and the qualities of Matisse's present interior appear in Vuillard's work only later. We are left then with a notably independent, if not especially adventurous, small-scale work. It establishes early in his career the fact that while Matisse continued throughout his lifetime to look for inspiration to the works of the past as well as of his contemporaries, he almost never succumbed to direct borrowing of manner or to the adaptation of another artist's composition. An exception to this rule is found in the Signac-inspired **Luxe, calme et volupté** (page 59) a decade later.

Painted 1900
Oil on canvas, 39 1/8 x 28 5/8 in.
The Museum of Modern Art, New York
Purchase

Male Model (L'Homme Nu, "Le Serf")

The especially monumental **Male Model**, or **Serf**, is one of the finest of the early works and is intimately related to his early explorations in sculpture, the bronze **Slave** being a companion work in that genre. There is a certain temptation to label this Matisse's "blue" period, thinking of a superficially similar phase that was shortly to overtake Picasso. However, the two artists' intentions are so radically opposed (nor had they met at the time) that it is misleading to use this label for Matisse's work, except in a very restricted way.

The painted version of the serf seems literally sculpted on the canvas, and the same is almost as true of the heavy swatches of blue, green, and ocher that form a far from neutral background. The planes of the body are brutal in their generality, as is the abruptness of their intersections in space. A remarkably intense contrast is formed between the high-hued yet somber interior and the highlights bathing most of the model's body. This contrast predicts certain color effects that Matisse would later achieve with pictures like the Shchukin version of **Dance** (page 73). In this early work such violent coloristic juxtaposition is moderated by the artist's intense concern for an illusion of bodily mass, with its receding and advancing planes of space. It is interesting to reflect that in works like this of about 1900, Matisse seems closer to a kind of Proto-Cubism than Picasso, whose works of the Blue Period were to stress expressive and pathetic arabesques rather than structural masses. Ironically, the two artists were to move in mutually contradictory directions in the evolution of their early careers: Picasso toward an increasingly ponderous figure style leading ultimately to the Demoiselles d'Avignon (1907) and Matisse toward an increasing reduction of the inner modeling of the figure, with a greater reliance on the shaping power of decorative arabesques and ringing color contrasts. Matisse achieved this evolution from boldly modeled to flattened figure structures in such mid-decade works as **Joy of Life** (1906), where even in the sketch (page 65) one perceives strong coloristic outlines of pale flesh tones that become penumbras, imaginary Fauvist shadows. This device is already detectable around the shoulders and back of **Male Model**, and is a device that Matisse seems to have invented in a pen-and-ink drawing of 1899 (figure 9), an unusual study of Delacroix's **Abduction of Rebecca** (1846), in which the highlighted figures are heavily surrounded by scrawls of black ink, an effect that Matisse superimposed on the Romantic master's original conception. So startling was this effect in the drawing that his fellow students in Moreau's atelier chided him for having made a "negative" (in the photographic sense) copy. However, this discovery would serve him well in the paintings of the next decade as he worked his way into an anti-Cubist style of rendering the figure.

Considering Matisse's subsequent fame as a figure painter, it is remarkable that through the first decade of his career major nude académies, whether male or female, are few in number in his work. It was not until 1900 that he undertook major figure studies, but then they quickly came to predominate.

Painted 1902
Oil on canvas, 24 3/4 x 31 1/8 in.
Pushkin Museum, Moscow

The Path in the Bois de Boulogne (Sentier, Bois de Boulogne)

If somewhat overshadowed by the great figure compositions, landscapes occupy an extremely important role at several moments in the artist's career. The present painting, with its dense foliage emphasized by the massive, almost Courbet-like facture, owes much to the study of Cézanne and thus complements Matisse's early efforts at monumental nudes in a Cézannesque manner. In fact, the present composition is closely related to one of the older artist's favorite motifs, the bend in a road leading to a village. Matisse's most notable change in this theme is that he selected a path in a park or garden rather than a simple country lane leading to a humble village, with all its implications of rustic toil (although there are, of course, notable exceptions to this observation: Cézanne's studies of avenues of trees at the Jas de Bouffan, his father's estate near Aix, for example). Given many of Matisse's later landscapes, including those framed by an open window, which are mainly of parks and gardens—that is to say, bits of cultivated, artificial paradise—the early appearance of this motif is particularly impressive. Moreover, this preference of Matisse's for nature in its cultivated state related closely to the evolution of an arcadian paradisial vision throughout his career.

Compared with the important series of small landscapes done by Matisse during his protracted stays in Corsica and Toulouse in 1898, paintings that are aptly denoted as Proto-Fauve, the color here is somber. The purple path and the stream at the right are these major features that hold everything together. Nevertheless, they are overshadowed by the frequently shapeless mass of foliage. Curiously un-Cézannesque is the absence of powerful intertwining limbs and twigs that might otherwise have given a more skeletal organization to the picture. These features are present as subject, but are never capitalized on as a dominant motif. This tentative rejection of one aspect of Cézanne's method of ordering things from a study of nature is, once again, a harbinger of the later landscapes, where foliage is rendered in broad, flat areas surrounded by arbitrary decorative arabesques, with only the barest indication of structural support from the limbs.

Painted 1903 (formerly dated 1902)
Oil on canvas, 21⅝ x 18⅛ in.
Reproduced by permission of the Syndics of the Fitzwilliam Museum,
Cambridge, England

The Attic Studio (Studio under the Eaves, L'Atelier sous les Toits)

This unusual, somewhat crudely executed interior was painted in the artist's makeshift studio atop his father's house at Bohain-en-Vermandois during a particularly trying period in his career. Economic distress had forced him to abandon Paris for a time. In its somber tones, accentuated rather than relieved by the small, luminous landscape glimpsed through the distant window, it, like other pictures of this epoch, looks back beyond the intense, saturated colors of his work in the late nineties to the earthen palette of his first efforts. On the other hand, its frontal composition, with vast expanses of vacant surface, abandons the diagonal or oblique axes of many earlier paintings, notably **La Desserte** (figure 7), as well as the self-portrait of 1900 (figure 1) and the majority of his figure studies of that epoch.

The flattening effect achieved by this spatial arrangement looks forward to the great studio series of 1911 (pages 77 and 79). Moreover, the theme of the open window, heretofore an accessory in his interiors if it appeared at all, is centralized and exploited for the first time in his work. It was a crucial motif that would occupy the artist until his last paintings on canvas, notably **Interior with Egyptian Curtain** (figure 53). Here, in fact, the window is made the thematic foil of the canvas which we see suspended from the easel in the middle distance. It would seem that the analogy between the picture frame and the frame of the window, each offering a controlled, measured fragment of the artist's world of appearances, finds its beginnings in this modest, unassuming canvas.

The theme of the open window had been thoroughly explored by German Romantic artists like Kaspar David Friedrich in the early nineteenth century, but its appearance in French art of that century was sporadic and incidental. Almost single-handedly, Matisse seems to have reinvented the significance if not the actual use of the open, uncurtained window and prepared the way for the exploitation of this theme by his contemporaries and juniors: Bonnard, Gris, Picasso, Delaunay, and even (ironically) Duchamp and Magritte. The play between two spaces, inner and outer, and the crucial analogy with the picture frame serve to define the universe of the artist. Without going to the extreme of tortuous allegories of sight, such as were employed by seventeenth-century Flemish painters like Jan Bruegel, Matisse makes a candid, factual statement concerning the artist's involvement with the subject. While the Impressionist painters, notably Pissarro in his late paintings of Paris done at the time Matisse met him in 1897, frequently painted from the vantage of an apartment window, they never indicated the interior or the frame of the window through which the artist was looking. Since 1900, Matisse had been studying the view of Notre-Dame and the Cité from his studio window on the Quai Saint-Michel, and this picture must be seen as a statement of his new interests.

Painted 1903
Oil on canvas, 31 1/2 x 25 1/4 in.
Museum of Fine Arts, Boston
Tompkins Collection, Arthur Gordon Tompkins Residuary Fund

Carmelina

If **The Attic Studio**, 1903, provides a startling glimpse into the future of Matisse's art during what seems to have been its darkest moment, then **Carmelina** is the undoubted though thoroughly conventional masterpiece of this somber period, which intervenes between his Proto-Fauve work of about 1897–1900 and his second excursion into Neo-Impressionism in 1904-5. A tightly cemented composition in which the parts mesh like perfectly functioning gears, it sums up the efforts of nineteenth-century realism. Its execution may well have helped Matisse to abandon certain insecurities concerning the styles of the past, which are revealed in his early works after moments of remarkable boldness. Compositionally, it makes an interesting comparison with the series of figure studies, both male and female, that were inaugurated in 1900, and of which **Male Model** (page 51) is a remarkable example. In those earlier works, which were as dominated by blue as **Carmelina** is dominated by ochers, the pictorial ground is handled with brutal abandon, the painted areas themselves creating vital supporting structures of their own. In this subsequent, regressive masterpiece the artist has had recourse to about every studio prop imaginable, and though their enumeration would not be as tedious as with the 1896 **Interior with Top Hat** (figure 5), its picturesque inventory stands in marked contrast to the swatches and patches of pure paint in **Male Model**. Could Matisse have been thinking of a Salon submission in the working out of **Carmelina**? It is one of his most rhetorical efforts in conventional compositional language. The body of the model merges with the draperies, and the roundness of her body works against the familiar rectangular foils of picture frames, a mirror, and drawings pinned to the wall. Tying the whole together is the startling contrast of lights and darks, particularly as they strike the robust, pliant body of the model, making of her figure something more stark and angular than it must have been in actuality. It is almost as if Corot, Courbet, and Cézanne had collaborated in the creation of a single canvas. Even the abrupt frontality of the pose does not mitigate its conventionality, and for this very reason the picture remains something of a puzzle in the context of Matisse's development in this decade. It suggests little of what was to follow in the next few years. In sum, it must be taken as a concept that the artist held in reserve for more than a decade, since he returned to this subject with frequency and enthusiasm only in the paintings and drawings of the 1920s and afterward.

Contrary to its conservative composition, **Carmelina** contains the germinal theme of the reflected mirror images of the artist and his model that would play such an important role in the second half of his career. Its importance for the future is thus iconographic; for the rest it is a profound scholarly summing up of received ideas.

Painted 1904 (sometimes dated 1904–5)
Oil on canvas, 37 x 46 in.
Private collection, Paris

Luxe, calme et volupté

In certain respects this calculating work can be considered an "apprentice" effort; in others it marks the beginning of a sonorous theme that reverberates through the artist's subsequent works almost to the very end. Hence it is a turning point of extraordinary consequence.

Its Neo-Impressionist style is contrived and stiff, and immediately proved uncongenial to Matisse's temperament, even though the palette featured here would continue in his Fauve works. In effect, it may be considered another experiment in the artist's early career—preparatory to his major innovations in **Joy of Life**.

The academic lifelessness of its manner is due to the influence of Signac and Cross. But if the style was somewhat self-defeating and, in effect, a betrayal of Matisse's freer, more personal and daring efforts of the years just before and after 1900, the subject was an ambitious anticipation of what was to follow in the next five decades.

An entire aesthetic is contained within the lines of this thrice-repeated refrain of Baudelaire's *L'Invitation au voyages*: "Là, tout nest qu'ordre et beauté, / Luxe, calme et volupté." Matisse did not seek a visual image to subsume the entire poem, but instead created a Cythera-like world out of the literal import and the onomatopoeic suggestiveness of these carefully selected words. In the foreground we discover a beach which recedes to the left, leaving an open bay at the right. That margin of the picture is secured by the trunk of a tree which, through certain spatially ambiguous, almost Cézannesque devices, is linked, in surface design, with the mast and boom of the beached boat in the middle distance. On this sandy shore a group of women are caught in a variety of indolent, relaxed attitudes. At the lower left a cloth is spread with the remains of a picnic, a detail reminiscent of certain early Cézanne compositions which are themselves filled with a tense, erotic suggestiveness. However, Matisse purges his work of these conflicts by maintaining a strictly female grouping, a calmness that he would ambiguously disrupt in the subsequent **Joy of Life**, with its conspicuous embracing couple in the right foreground.

There is, of course, much in the way of mechanical technique to admire in this stilted composition. The dark shading behind the standing figure nearest the tree at the right and the greenish shadows cast beneath the seated and reclining figures predict a bolder use of the same device in later works. True, the labored brushwork and forced tensions between spatial illusion and surface design will give way to a greater spontaneity in **Joy of Life**. Nonetheless, Matisse's skill in mastering a style that is, strictly speaking, someone else's commands more than mere respect. He could have remained simply a gifted eclectic and still have found his place in the history of early modern painting. As it was, he had another destiny.

Painted 1905
Oil on canvas, 16 x 12 3/4 in.
The Royal Museum of Fine Arts, Copenhagen
J. Rump Collection

The Green Stripe (Madame Matisse, Portrait à la Raie Verte)

The modest dimensions of this canvas are surprising, for its impact is monumental, owing to the astute balance of totally saturated colors. The green stripe down the nose is theoretically supported not by the contours of the cheeks but by the blue green of the collar. Yet if this axis, together with the densely painted flesh tones, were the sole support of the blue-black crown of hair, the pictorial structure would collapse. Stubbornly, all these features are kept securely fixed in space through the intense, luminous orange, violet, and green surroundings. Few Fauve canvases are so completely supported by color alone as is this portrait of the artist's wife. Furthermore, the unity of the head and the sustaining color areas (it is almost out of the question to refer to them as a "background") is maintained by a unique crisscross blend in the flesh tones. The left side of the face tends to echo the green of the picture's right, the corresponding being true for the right side, where the more forthrightly pink skin responds to the orange of the left.

In spite of these rarefied, boldly brushed coloristic effects, we nonetheless sense the artist's determination to fashion a likeness. In contrast to Cézanne in many of his late portraits, Matisse is not content with a study of planes and structures, leaving us with a masklike impression. In his contemporary **Woman with Hat**, the artist employs a similar palette, but as the color still remains somewhat broken in that particular portrait of his wife, the effect is less concise. Similarly, in that painting the immediate presence of the model is less strongly communicated, and thus we are left with the belief that **The Green Stripe** offers a more accurate and penetrating likeness. However, if Matisse has used color here to the maximum of its expressive and connotative possibilities, he has not produced an image of Expressionistic psychology. The dignified bearing and assured manner of the model are communicated without the slightest ambiguity, and in the end we realize that these abrupt juxtapositions of saturated pigment result from the calculated pictorial decisions of an artist possessed of a unique skill in the balance and contrast of color.

Painted 1905
Oil on canvas, 21 3/4 x 18 1/8 in.
Collection Mr. and Mrs. John Hay Whitney, New York

Open Window, Collioure (La Fenêtre, Fenêtre Ouverte)

This is the grand classic statement of the open window as a crucial formal and conceptual theme in Matisse's art, and one of the central masterpieces of the short-lived Fauve movement. This and other pictures of the period mark Matisse's final liberation from the constraints of Neo-Impressionism. Moreover, in this nearly symmetrical picture, with its flanking, framing areas of intense blue green and electrifying pink, the artist had a format in which he could work out the problem of broad, maximized areas of color. The theme of the landscape seen through the open window (here a harbor view), even more emphatically a picture within a picture than in **The Attic Studio** (page 55), carries on in the artist's work, culminating in the remarkable **Interior with Egyptian Curtain** (figure 53). One further compositional device must be mentioned: the variously colored rectangular shapes of the individual panes of glass and the supplementary rectangles of the transom must be compared with certain details of the early studio interiors such as **Interior with Top Hat** (figure 5) and **Carmelina** (page 57). Now the artist has emphatically drawn the theme of the picture within a picture to new, virtually symbolic levels. The reflective and translucent panes of glass, vibrantly colored, now supplant the more prosaic pictures and frames on the walls of the earlier interiors. In effect, each of these patches of color, whether pale or intense, can be read as an individual miniature and as a structured part of a coherent whole. Finally, Matisse's lifelong predilection for nature in its cultivated aspects, first hinted at in **The Path in the Bois de Boulogne** three years earlier (page 53), is underscored in the rectangular garland of ivy clinging to the balcony just beyond the open windows.

The striking color juxtapositions have excited such interest in this picture that the more thoughtful qualities of its palette are often missed. Note the contrasting symmetrical pillars of green and pink, and the tendency of the window panes to reflect chiefly the hue of the opposite side. Alfred Barr has justly commented on the inconsistencies of brushwork between the interior and exterior, finding a certain Impressionistic survival in the conception of the latter (*Matisse*, p. 72). But this difference is to a degree functional, serving to demarcate two distinct worlds. Moreover, the broken brush strokes of the exterior serve to thrust emphatically forward and thus render more intense the flat passages serving as framing elements. Indeed, the relatively long strokes of the exterior resemble Impressionist technique less than they resemble many Matisses from the Nice epoch of 1917 and afterward. The one paradox, intentional or not, is that the artist has here produced a picture in which the frame is more important than the view.

Painted 1906 (sometimes dated 1905)
Oil on canvas, 16 1/8 x 21 5/8 in.
Private collection, San Francisco

Sketch for Joy of Life (Joie de Vivre)

The present study is the most developed of three preparatory oils for the monumental final version, almost eight feet wide, in the Barnes Foundation (figure 4). This arcadian conception follows directly out of the earlier picture **Luxe, calme et volupté** (page 59), and is both a reaction and a further creative response to Matisse's preoccupations of the recent past with a variety of new movements. While the study indicates an indebtedness to Neo-Impressionist style in certain of its areas, these references are banished in the broadly brushed final version. While the studies and final version mark the epitome of the artist's work as a Fauve, the final version in particular heralds the development in his subsequent work of large, abruptly juxtaposed flat areas of thinly brushed, high-keyed color, a tendency that was pursued through the monumental works of the teens and thirties and culminates with the last *papiers-découpés* of the early fifties.

Analogies can profitably be made with some of the great pictures of the sixteenth-century Venetians, notably Titian's **Bacchanal**. Another and more recent comparison is Ingres's **Golden Age**, where the circle of dancers is to be found in the foreground. However, historians have tended to relate this picture to a near contemporary, Picasso's **Demoiselles d'Avignon**, of 1907, and while they occupy parallel stages in the careers of their respective artists, the profound differences in the aims of the two men at this time preclude drawing many conclusions from so abrupt a confrontation. More to the point might be a comparison with Cézanne's **Large Bathers** (Philadelphia), finished in 1905, which Matisse just possibly could have seen at Vollard's. The dimensions of the two canvases are remarkably similar, and the scale of the figures is also comparable. Matisse's sinuous contours in the sheltering bower of trees in **Joy of Life** could well be a response to the sternly, architectural feature of the bent tree limbs in Cézanne's painting. Iconographically, Matisse's masterpiece perhaps owes something to Signac's 1895 composition **Le Temps d'harmonie**, a terrestrial paradise in contemporary costume and with a working-class orientation, which nonetheless features a round of dancers under a tree in the distance. Another, more closely associated picture is Derain's **Golden Age**, dated about 1905, where the theme is strikingly similar but the treatment more violent and the scale of the figures larger. Matisse and Derain worked on these related arcadian subjects simultaneously and could have exchanged ideas. A further revealing juxtaposition can be made with Edvard Munch's figure paintings, dating back as far as 1890, which show a totally different, pessimistic and despairing attitude toward the earthly paradise.

In sum, Matisse's painting represents a fusion of several important trends in late nineteenth-century art, as well as an anticipation of many things to come in his own work.

Painted 1907
Oil on canvas, 82 3/4 x 54 3/8 in.
Musée National d'Art Moderne, Paris

Le Luxe I

This picture, a full-size study for the final version in Copenhagen (figure 19), is undoubtedly more "interesting" to the critic preoccupied with the evolution of Matisse's art. However, it is infinitely less complete than the more articulate, simplified, and compact statement of **Le Luxe II**, which remains one of the artist's most serene images. Iconographically a condensation of **Luxe, calme et volupté** (page 59), its two major figures, the statuesque but hardly sculptural standing figure and the one crouching at her feet, actually derive from the two figures to the left of **Joy of Life**. The crouching figure has now been reversed, and the standing one here lowers her arms. The image of Lesbos, already present in Matisse's Neo-Impressionist composition and even in **Joy of Life**, is here made more explicit with the gesture of the bouquet-bearing figure hurrying in from the right. Indeed, Matisse would develop this concept further in the small **Music (Sketch)** (figure 20), with the embracing couple, both female, dancing to the music of the solitary male violinist. Parallel themes reappear in numerous drawings and a few paintings from the 1920s and 1930s. Here, in **Le Luxe I**, Baudelaire's verses, especially "Là, tout n'est qu'ordre et beauté," seem more fully realized than before, with the repetition of the theme of a world in which the male figure, with all its implications, is banished. Indeed, from this point onward, the appearance of the male nude is rare in Matisse's work, and except for the final **Music** (page 75), his role is usually the predatory one of the satyr.

Le Luxe I contains many powerful features that had to be sacrificed in order to reach the expressive heights of the final version. Even the barest survival here and there of a brush stroke suggestive of Impressionism indicates the reluctance with which Matisse was shedding many of the received and learned techniques of his youth. The penumbras surrounding the figures, seen earlier, are virtually gone in the sketch, save for the back of the flower girl, and do not appear at all in the final version. And his most brilliant color concept, the pale copper-oxide blue green of the kneeling figure, had to be ruthlessly omitted from the final version for it to attain its unique serenity. In effect, Matisse here gives us a modern Aphrodite risen from the sea, erotic yet narcissistic, destined for the eyes and supplications of her own sex. It is a developed and expanded fragment of **Joy of Life**, just as, three years later, **Dance** (page 73) was destined to be. In **Le Luxe I** the artist offers us more than a hint of his consummate skill as a draftsman, in close conjunction with his adroitly controlled genius in contrasting colors for a maximum of expressive and poetic effect. The stylized arabesques of the figures in **Le Luxe I** and their fluent, almost life size contours map the direction of Matisse's immediate future and point the way to his decorative, architecturally scaled works of the 1930s and later.

Painted 1907
Oil on canvas, 28 3/4 x 23 5/8 in.
Private collection, United States

Landscape with Brook (Brook with Aloes)

Scenes painted from nature were of extreme importance in Matisse's early evolution, especially as he liberated himself from his earlier dark manner, first in the Breton trips of 1895–97 and then in his year spent in the south in 1898. Subsequently, in **The Path in the Bois de Boulogne** (page 53), he sought to assimilate certain aspects of Cézanne's structure into his then formative style. The present picture, contemporary with the great figure pieces of the period, notably **Le Luxe I** and **II**, demonstrates how his newfound compositional design could be applied to the study of landscape. While not yet displaying the lyrical simplicity of the later Tangier scenes (for example, page 85), the artist has already found a personal, unique post-Fauve vision of nature, one that supplements as well as reinforces the major tendencies of his larger, virtually mythological paintings of the period 1906–10. The surface pattern is here the chief structural device, and color is the vehicle whereby it is accomplished. The brook flows across the front of the scene, but does not lead us back into an illusionistic space. The hillside of greens, blues, and ochers offers a soft harmony of hues that is barely disturbed by a few impetuously Fauve touches of red. Furthermore, the high horizon reinforces the picture's lack of depth, leading the eye upward rather than inward. Clearly this is a transitional painting with a few minor and undisturbing inconsistencies, as in the rather heavily painted surface of the water. However, it is an important landmark in the evolution of a motif in Matisse's art that is often overlooked. True, after the twenties, landscapes are rare in his work. But the theme of nature is subsequently transposed in his final designs, emerging in such visions as **The Lagoon**, one of the most abstract of the plates from *Jazz* (1947), or the monumental decorative composition **Parakeet and Siren** (1952), one of his most abstract transformations of nature. In effect, the seeds for those culminating interpretations of foliage were planted as early as the present picture.

Painted 1909
Oil on canvas, 69 3/4 x 85 7/8 in.
The Hermitage, Leningrad

Harmony in Red (La Desserte Rouge, Harmonie Rouge)

The monumentality of this ambitious still life looks backward to **La Desserte** (figure 7) and anticipates **Still Life with Aubergines** (page 83). This series of pictures indicates Matisse's ambition to develop in large format a motif that is customarily treated in a more intimate fashion. At this point in his career, with so much of his effort dedicated to large-scale figure compositions, Matisse clearly felt the need to achieve something equivalent in another, time-honored theme of Western art, one which, a century before, had not been considered worthy of the same attention from artists as large figure paintings or even portraiture. Hence, **Harmony in Red** is one of the artist's major contributions to the equalization and democratization of hierarchies in subject matter.

The magnetic red of the wall and tablecloth, with the interweaving blue pattern, is one of Matisse's most unusual color creations, and its history is fascinating and complex. The canvas began its life as **Harmony in Green** (the landscape through the window is almost certainly a survival of this stage), and was then transformed into **Harmony in Blue** in 1908. It was publicly exhibited in this second state, and sold to Sergei Shchukin, who apparently intended it to be a decorative panel for his dining room. Then, in 1909, Matisse persuaded Shchukin to return the picture to him, and at that time the definitive **Harmony in Red** emerged. The fact that he was working on a predominantly blue ground rather than on a fresh white canvas very likely influenced him in his choice of this particular red. To judge from photographs of the intermediate stage of the picture, the effect was always flat, the surface of the table and the perpendicular wall behind being treated in a similar, continuous fashion so that the rear surface enjoys a clear unity with the picture plane. The landscape seen through the window at the upper left reinforces the floral arabesques of the interior, setting up a provocative dialogue between nature itself and its decorative transformations found in the interior. Nevertheless, the landscape is itself stylized, providing a premonition of the kind of design that Matisse would employ in his Tangier landscapes four years later. Looking backward, **Harmony in Red** is a vast advance over **La Desserte**. The high diagonal view of the earlier picture is here replaced by an approximate frontality. In producing one of his most flattened, tapestry-like works of that date, Matisse employed an extraordinarily conventional if almost invisible underpinning of Renaissance perspective, reaching back behind the innovations and distortions employed by artists of the previous century. While we may regret the disappearance of two other paintings beneath the final layer of the finished version, there can be little doubt that what we now see is a vastly more intense composition, one which perhaps could not exist in quite the way it presently does without the sacrifice of the earlier pictures in green and blue.

Painted 1910
Oil on canvas, 101⅝ x 153½ in.
The Hermitage, Leningrad

Dance

This painting may be interpreted as an anti-Cubist demonstration of how figures may be linked by means of muscular arabesques and intense color contrasts with the abstracted ground, in contrast to Cubism's evolving device of binding together figures and objects through arbitrary overlaps and planar deformations in an illusionistic space. Its mural-like size was perhaps inevitable, given the expanding scale toward which the artist was then moving, but the happy coincidence of a commission for a series of decorative compositions for the Moscow mansion of the Russian merchant Sergei Shchukin surely goaded the artist along. A full-size study (The Museum of Modern Art, New York), whose pale flesh tones did not attempt to reach the saturation point achieved by the terra-cotta ochers of the final version, indicates that the artist was here proceeding in a way analogous to **Le Luxe I**.

Dance was conceived as part of a series of three monumental compositions, to be followed by **Music** (page 75) and **Bathers by the River** (page 97). But only **Dance** and **Music** were completed at the time; a small study of five bathers exists (figure 21), and in 1917 the artist completed **Bathers by the River** in a paradoxically Neo-Cubist style.

The sources for **Dance** are multiple, reaching back into antiquity (maenad figures on Greek vases; Graeco-Roman images of the Three Graces). Matisse furthermore told interviewers that he had been stimulated by observing country dancers at Collioure and Parisians dancing at the Moulin de la Galette, an indication that he kept his eye on contemporary life while developing his modern mythologies. The pale, realistic, flesh tones of the five women in the full-size sketch of **Dance** give way in the final version to a violent red-ocher suggestive of red-figure Greek vases, with the result that a highly saturated contrast is achieved with the green ground and blue sky. Several crucial lines are strengthened in the definitive canvas, emphasizing the tensions and relaxations of movement. The hands of the figures at the left and in the foreground are brought closer together, creating a tension of contact rivaling Michelangelo's **Creation of Man**.

Matisse here poses a major aesthetic problem—the relation of the design to the image—in a way that he had never done before with such emphasis. This forceful tension between the image and the design is complemented by the stark contrast of positive figural solid and negative spatial void. Given that at this moment the pioneer Cubists, Picasso and Braque, were developing a style that blurred when it did not disrupt the familiar boundaries between solid and void, Matisse's style here emerges as strikingly anti-Cubist.

Painted 1910
Oil on canvas, 101 5/8 x 153 1/2 in.
The Hermitage, Leningrad

Music

This last time that Matisse turned his attention to a composition of male figures (their genitalia were subsequently painted out, probably at the insistence of the client) he reduced them to a series of hieroglyphs, but, significantly, musical ones. One of his most challenging inventions, it remains explicable only in terms of the dancers that preceded and the bathers that were to follow (but which were not realized until six years later, and in another mode). And yet in the stasis of this present sequence of music makers he has produced a disposition unique even in his own work—the only possible release from the preceding round of dancers. There is no consistent precedent for identifying dance with the female and music with the male; indeed, as the pictures presently stand, the sexual differentiation may be virtually meaningless.

Originally, to judge from two photographs made while the picture was in progress (figures 22 and 23; apparently there were no preliminary versions), the composition was less rigid. In fact, the compositional changes may still be detected today beneath the final painting. A far cry from the muscular, faceted studio models of ten years before, yet coloristically related, these five figures attest once again to Matisse's insistent simplification of a given problem as he worked at it over the years. Thematically, **Music** is connected with a slightly earlier, more provocative work of the same title of about 1907 (figure 20), where the violinist at the left presides over a scene in which two embracing women dance while a male figure serves as *repoussoir* in the right foreground. Hardly a study for the present picture, it nonetheless links the themes of **Music** and **Dance** at a slightly earlier stage in the artist's career. The pipe player, second from left in the 1910 **Music**, evokes a recumbent figure from **Joy of Life**, but for the rest this is a unique effort. The evolutionary changes which affect chiefly the three figures to the right lead to a bold frontality. In the completed picture they become, as it were, notes on a staff of music (as does the pipe player), with the increasingly rigid violinist doing service as a kind of treble clef.

Painted 1911
Oil on canvas, 71 1/4 x 86 1/4 in.
The Museum of Modern Art, New York
Mrs. Simon Guggenheim Fund

Red Studio (L'Atelier Rouge, Le Panneau Rouge)

achievements of artists like Barnett Newman and Mark Rothko. Here the past of realistic studio interiors by Courbet, Bazille, and others merges with the present of concern for color-field painting or for exploring the threshold of visual perception. The nature of its "redness" is itself magical, utterly without precedent in other paintings by Matisse. The physical surface is matte and dry, the spatial effect is barely suggested, the local colors of individual objects (many themselves paintings) play almost no role in the total effect, and the final impression is both electric and inducive of contemplation. It is an allegory of the senses, both as a pure painted surface and as a representation of a corner of the artist's studio filled with objects of obvious biographic significance. Matisse was uniquely placed in the chronology of recent art to bring all these contradictory concepts together simultaneously, but he was also uniquely equipped in temperament (in terms of where he had started and where he was destined to end) to be the human bridge across which such contacts could be made.

Intensely monochromatic, it seems in retrospect a reflection and perhaps even a criticism of Cubism's similar tendencies at the time, since it employs a high- rather than low-key tonality. Spatially, of course, nothing could be further removed from the paradoxes of Cubism than this stenographic tapestry-like study of the artist's working environment, a theme that reaches back to his earliest endeavors. The composition is casual and almost indifferent. Gone are the close interweavings and the tying together of one object to another through either surface or spatial overlapping. Instead, the space opens out into a hitherto unseen infinity, one which always returns us to the surface of the painting proper, providing a unique atmosphere which forms the setting for discrete objects, thus insuring each its own importance and dignity. Once one is past the redness of this picture, its individual elements take on a life of their own, and in a topographic situation that remains realistically convincing.

What is absent from this study of the artist's environment is the artist's model or the artist himself, elements that will appear later in paintings and in countless drawings. The space is empty and uninhabited, except by its special tone, and it is there that we may detect not just an atmosphere but the particular mind and taste of Matisse. Later studio pictures may be more genial, suggestive, and picturesque, but in a grander sense his presence is contained in this image to a greater degree than ever again in a rendering of a similar motif.

Moreover, as a document pure and simple, **Red Studio** contains a summary rendering in the left corner of a lamentably destroyed work, **Large Nude with Necklace**, whose major tonality points to **Red Studio**'s companion piece, **Pink Studio** (page 79).

The very simplicity of its hue masks one of the artist's most subtle achievements, a composition that remains a paragon of contemporary art even after the passage of time and the

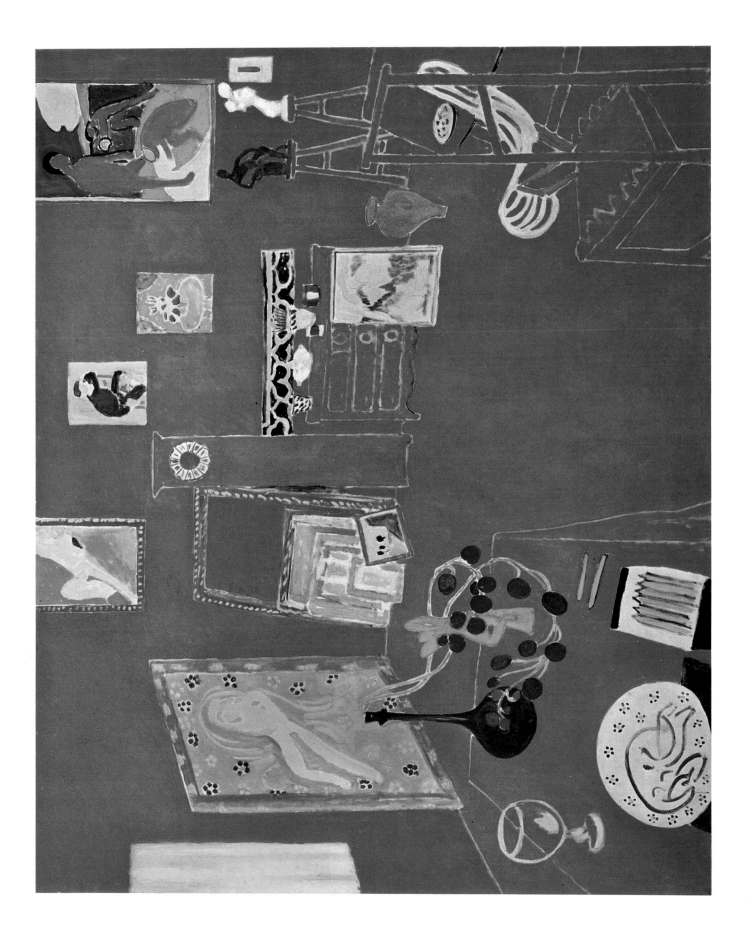

Painted 1911
Oil on canvas, 69 3/4 x 82 1/4 in.
Pushkin Museum, Moscow

Pink Studio
(The Painter's Studio,
L'Atelier Rose)

The first impression received from this picture is as jolting as that of its companion, **Red Studio** (previous page). The unheralded quality of the pink, which is not as all-pervasive as the red of the other, is in no way muted by the differing intensities applied to the floor and the wall, and the prominent areas of green and blue serve to reinforce its sumptuous luminosity, a quality significantly absent from **Red Studio**.

The topography of the studio is here more explicit; the view, with its glimpse through the open window—a motif recaptured from the earlier **The Attic Studio** (page 55)—is conventionally frontal, whereas **Red Studio** looks more obliquely into a corner. That both of these monumental compositions were painted in the same environment, the artist's studio at Issy-les-Moulineaux, is demonstrated by the correspondence of several works of art, notably the second version of **Le Luxe**, indicating that the right third of **Red Studio** is in actuality the left third of **Pink Studio**. That the artist could sequentially compose two such strikingly contrasting yet equally intense color studies of his actual working environment is astounding, and illustrates the degree to which the reality of the picture's unique being had taken control of his art by 1911. Both are paintings about painting, through their demonstrations of post-Fauve color control, but they further indicate the artist's newfound satisfaction with his immediate surroundings as a motif to create a buoyant world of the imagination as satisfying and idyllic as **Joy of Life** and subsequent expansions on that theme. One has only to compare these works with earlier studio pictures to realize the degree to which the artist has now rediscovered the nature and pictorial potential of his working environment, finding it no longer necessary to invent a mythological world as the thematic skeleton for the exploration of color and line. The slightly sordid, untidy appearance of the earlier studio pictures is now gone for good.

The sumptuousness of **Pink Studio** offers, on prolonged contemplation, a more mellow air; one becomes accustomed to its haunting atmosphere in a way that contrasts absolutely with the sustained, unrelenting **Red Studio**. A chordal harmony rather than a long-sustained single note is present here, and in spite of its monumentality and the grandeur of its central parts, it prepares us for the small-scale interiors of the 1920s. The analogy between this painting and Courbet's **Atelier** (1854–55), is more striking, but once again the artist's presence is not actually seen, but only felt through the wizardry of his color.

Painted 1911
Oil on canvas, 56 1/4 x 76 3/8 in.
The Hermitage, Leningrad

The Painter's Family

(page 73 and previous page) were painted in his workrooms constructed in the garden and **Still Life with Aubergines** (page 83) shows us the interior of his villa at Collioure. Hence, these four pictures sum up the artist's life and surroundings of that year, before he temporarily extended his working environment to North Africa.

This is the only one of the four pictures to introduce the figure. His wife is in the left distance, his sons Pierre and Jean are at the checkerboard, and his daughter, Marguerite, stands at the right. The overall flatness of design, relieved and contradicted by certain perspective details, corresponds to the technique of the other three. However, the quality of the color, predominantly red and red-brown, lacks the ringing, sonic quality of the others. While not muted, the color is static, a feature helped by Marguerite's black dress. A single work of art, a small bronze figure, stands on the mantel over the central fireplace. Otherwise this is a domestic, bourgeois interior and, despite the picture's large size, remarkably Intimist in quality. Indeed, it suggests comparison with Vuillard's monumental decorative project for the library of Dr. Vaquez, **Personnages dans des Intérieurs** (1896), which was publicly exhibited for the first time at the 1905 Autumn Salon, the same which contained the "cage of wild beasts," and it is likely that Matisse saw it at that time. Matisse had met Vuillard much earlier, and had known of his work from about 1897, but curiously was little interested at the time in the efforts of the Nabis, of whom Vuillard was a member. In fact, Matisse's career through its first two decades was moving in a direction counter to that of Vuillard. It is just possible, however, that by 1911 Matisse was prepared to integrate Intimist themes, and even touches of their style, into his work. It is noteworthy that he later became a close friend of the other great Nabi master, Pierre Bonnard. Concerning the checkerboard theme, one should remember that it was employed by Cubist painters at this time, notably by Juan Gris, whose acquaintance Matisse was to make at Collioure in the summer of 1914. Further afield, it is interesting to speculate on the artist's choice of a game of checkers as the central, unifying theme of this domestic interior. Employing a different game played on the same board, namely chess, Marcel Duchamp had already treated the subject pictorially and by 1911 was exploring the metaphysical connotations of chess players in his **King and Queen Surrounded by Swift Nudes**. This stretched comparison only serves to underscore the materialistic and mythological, as opposed to the metaphysical, sources of Matisse's art. However idealized, spiritualized, and abstract his paintings became, his point of departure was always the real world of immediate sensations, a real world that became increasingly sumptuous as time passed.

This is another of the four great "Symphonic Interiors" (to borrow Alfred Barr's apt phrase), perhaps the third of the series to be completed. It was painted in the artist's villa at Issy-les-Moulineaux, whereas **Red Studio** and **Pink Studio**

Painted 1911
Tempera on canvas, 82 3/4 x 96 1/8 in.
Musée de Peinture et de Sculpture, Grenoble

Still Life with Aubergines

The title of this picture is a monumental understatement, and one wonders if the artist used it ironically. It is, in terms of accessories and devices, one of the most complete presentations of his ongoing fundamental theme, the conversion of the artist's own studio into the idyllic world of **Joy of Life**. This was a personal and artistic quest lasting a lifetime, and it would be unreasonable to expect that one single canvas could sum it all up. Still lacking here is the literal presence of the model and of the artist, but by the time we encounter these phenomena in the smaller-scale, more intimate works of the 1920s, the grandeur of this design would be beyond Matisse, at least momentarily, if only because he was concentrating on more delicately nuanced phenomena of vision and subject.

An inventory of this picture is mandatory. Three aubergines are balanced precariously on a table whose red cloth carries an undulating white pattern that reinforces their tuberous shape. A mirror at the left, partly obscured at the bottom by a drawing portfolio, reflects these and other objects on the table in an inconsistent fashion. It is as if Matisse is stating that the artist's mirror image of nature in a painting may take certain licenses with reality in the interests of the picture itself. That it is indeed a mirror, and not another painting within a painting, is demonstrated by the reflection of part of the folding screen with floral pattern that occupies the center of the composition. Behind the screen we glimpse the top of an open door, probably leading to another room, where our eye is arrested by a checkered blue hanging. On the wall to the right is an open window with a real landscape beyond. For the rest, the floor and the wall are covered with abstract five-part floral patterns, all identical; this uniformity of the horizontal and vertical planes sets up a key surface tension with the illusion of spatial depth, a depth that opens both outward and inward (through the mirror reflection) along three separate diagonal axes. Originally the picture carried a painted frame several inches in breadth, with the identical floor-wall pattern, thus heightening the effect of decorative continuity and further reducing the scale of the aubergines themselves; unfortunately, this has been barbarically cut away. The total effect of the picture is one of an imaginary landscape constructed of a studio interior, since the space is as rich in floral abundances as it is in conventional studio props. Thus for the present Matisse completes, at vast scale, his allegory of the artist's world, seen here more emphatically than before as a garden of paradise. His well-known admiration for Persian miniatures, many of which illustrate actual gardens of delight, is here sublimated into a major theme of Western art, one that is central to Matisse's creative odyssey.

Painted 1912
Oil on canvas, 46 x 32 in.
Florene M. Schoenborn-Samuel A. Marx Collection, New York

Moroccan Garden (Pervenches)

Like many nineteenth- and twentieth-century painters, Matisse traveled a great deal: to Germany, Italy, Spain, Russia, the United States, and even to the South Pacific. Yet one would not think of him as an itinerant painter in the same sense as Corot, the Barbizon masters, or even the Impressionists and Post-Impressionists. He certainly observed both art and nature during these trips, but he only infrequently worked on the road. He was not the sort of artist who went searching anywhere and everywhere for motifs to stimulate a restless imagination; he carried most of his themes within him.

An exception to this rule is to be found in his experiences of North Africa during the winters of 1911–12 and 1912–13, and both trips were extraordinarily productive in terms of range and quantity. During the first trip he produced what was in effect a triptych of garden paintings from the park in Tangier. A powerful study in intense pink, blue, purple, and green, **Park in Tangier** (figure 25), is one of the companions to the present, more refined composition. While the Stockholm version represents the artist's more immediate response to a new environment, this picture, with its nuances of color contrast and more lyrical design, deserves to be compared with some of his earlier, more abstract work, notably the landscape of **Blue Window** (figure 24), or even the glimpse of the outdoors in the upper right of **Still Life with Aubergines** (previous page). In short, Matisse has quickly integrated his perceptions of a new and unfamiliar environment with his habitual matured manner of structuring a landscape. The rose of the sky is joined to the greens of the foreground through the color and structure of the tree trunk, and the foliage is rendered in large patches held together in the distance by billowing arabesques. These in turn contrast with the few specific, individual leaves that are summarily indicated in the foreground. The distance covered between **The Path in the Bois de Boulogne** (page 53) and this **Moroccan Garden** of precisely a decade later is enormous. The route that was traversed can be seen not only in landscape paintings per se but in the many glimpses of exteriors seen through open windows. Moreover, the decorative discipline of these studies of nature is no less than that found in his interiors of the same epoch.

Painted 1912
Oil on canvas, 45 5/8 x 39 3/8 in.
Pushkin Museum, Moscow

Zorah on the Terrace (Sur la Terrasse)

It was as if Matisse had at last accepted Baudelaire's *Invitation au voyage*—the source of **Luxe, calme et volupté** (page 59)—when he undertook his two working trips to Tangier during 1911–13. Nor can these trips to a Muslim environment be dissociated from his profound appreciation of Persian art. It was as if he were seeking to reinforce artistic experiences through a real confrontation with a nature and a people foreign to normal European experience. At the same time, thanks to the internal development of his own art culminating in **Still Life with Aubergines** (page 83), he was exactly at the point of being maximally prepared for the experience, so that it reinforced rather than diverted the creative path on which he had embarked during the previous decade. One thinks immediately of Delacroix's parallel experience in 1832 and the long-standing repercussions of that trip on his art.

With this crouching study of the Tangier model, Zorah, whom the artist had rendered standing as the center panel of a triptych the previous winter, Matisse once again creates the centerpiece of a new tripartite composition (the right wing, **Entrance to the Kasbah**, is reproduced in the next colorplate). The present study of Zorah thrusts us into a world tantalizingly parallel to that of Delacroix's **Women of Algiers** (1834), but with significant differences. Whereas Delacroix conjures up the closed, shadowy world of the harem interior, with opulent surroundings (much as Matisse would suggest with the odalisques of the 1920s), Matisse places his model outside, on a rooftop under blazing sunlight, with a minimum of accessories. But the intensity of the light is muted by a pale green shadow that supports this color in Zorah's dress, much as the blue of the carpet functions for the lower part of her dress. The pink patch of sunlight in the upper left is balanced by a matching hue in the goldfish bowl in the lower right. Thus the principle of cross-correspondence of color found in his Fauvist work—notably **The Green Stripe** (page 61)—recurs in a post-Fauve effort. As for the goldfish bowl, an element curiously out of context here, it is simply a reference to a motif that the artist was currently exploring in many different versions in his studio. In effect, given its placement, we might think of the goldfish as Matisse's monogrammed signature to this picture.

Painted 1912
Oil on canvas, 45 5/8 x 31 1/2 in.
Pushkin Museum, Moscow

Entrance to the Kasbah (La Porte de la Kasbah)

This painting is the right wing of the triptych that the artist produced during his second trip to Tangier, one made in the company of his old Fauve comrades, Marquet and Camoin. Although there is a sketchily realized seated figure in the shadow at the left; the picture is almost exclusively concerned with rendering a tightly defined architectural space as seen under the violent contrasts of light and shade typical of North Africa. The colors function accordingly. The blue circle of sky is barely distinguishable from the blue of the arched passage. The blue shadows of the foreground are only slightly more saturated, perhaps chiefly to support the intense pitch of the pink stream of sunlight on the pavement. At first glance this "keyhole" motif seems unique in the artist's work, until we realize that it is a special variant on the idea of the landscape or view seen through a window; this latter theme is actually the subject of Window at Tangier, the left-hand panel of this triptych. In that picture we are offered a broad panorama of the city, perhaps from the artist's hotel room, whereas here the view beyond is constricted with respect to both width and depth. The color relationships between the three pictures are especially interesting. The darker blues of the left panel suggest the murkiness of interior shadows; the green of the central panel behind the model, Zorah, suggests the half-light of a partly shaded exterior; and the intense luminosity of **Entrance to the Kasbah**, farthest to the right, illustrates the unrelieved power of the tropical sun reflecting on building exteriors. The movement from left to right is one of darkness to light, which in effect becomes the subject of the whole ensemble. Although each painting has its own distinctive coloration, there are subtle points of contact joining the three together in a unified way. Through the decade the idea of the triptych recurs in Matisse's work: in addition to the Amido-Zorah-Fatma series of the previous winter, there is the splendid **Three Sisters** (figure 32), in which three models are posed in different costume in three varied compositions in each of the panels, resulting in a grand total of nine figures alternately standing or seated.

Painted 1913
Oil on canvas, 57 7/8 x 38 1/4 in.
The Hermitage, Leningrad

Madame Matisse

This likeness stands in stark contrast to the Fauve **The Green Stripe** (page 61), and so far as hue is concerned illustrates the extremes that are possible in Matisse's art in the space of less than a decade. Its monochromatic insistency is not so great as in the nearly contemporary **Blue Window** (figure 24), nor are the blues precisely the same, but both pictures represent a severely restrained decorative impulse, always present with the artist, pushed to an archaistic extreme. The masklike face is modeled in gray, and the features are picked out by a series of curved lines that structurally relate to the general shape of the head. The blue-suited body is flattened, its contours closely related to the green outline of the wicker chair. The play of blue and green, the former dominating, is accented by an orange stole, which likewise relates on the left side to the vertical of the chair and body arm but on the right cuts across it. Its function is largely to prevent the disappearance of the figure in the relatively uniform blue background, which gives no hint as to specific environment. In this respect, the pure painted ground employed to set off the figure resembles in principle the ground of **The Green Stripe**. In other respects, however, the relationship between figure and surroundings could not be more opposed. The sense of volume that is produced by the contrasting colors of the earlier picture is here largely reversed, in spite of the part played by the orange stole, and the figure and background threaten to merge into a kind of premature field painting.

There are several other portraits of this period to which **Madame Matisse** should be compared, notably **Mlle. Yvonne Landsberg** (figure 30) of 1914, in which the heart-shaped motif of the body is reinforced by concentric contours to create a unique decorative effect of illusionary transparent planes bearing at least an accidental relationship to one of Cubism's cardinal constructive devices. Also, in **Mlle. Yvonne Landsberg** the masklike quality of the face is carried a step further. Another significant comparison is with the contemporary portraits of Derain.

Painted 1914–15
Oil on canvas, 57 1/2 x 38 1/4 in.
Collection Marcel Mabille, Brussels

Composition: The Yellow Curtain

One of the climactic instances of Matisse's treatment of the view through an open window, the present picture presents a daringly abstract landscape and frame which are contrasted with the relatively realistic handling of the curtain at the left. The green areas of the architectural border are so flatly treated that the landscape beyond is almost literally a picture within a picture and might even be read as a boldly simplified painting hanging on a studio wall. The curtain is actually red with a green floral pattern, and its reverse side, yellow, is seen only in two places where it has fluttered back into the room as the result of a breeze. Its yellow is nearly identical to the yellow-ocher ground of the landscape, a broad, flatly painted area which vibrates against two areas of relatively pale blue, the sky at the top and the elliptical form at the bottom, an area that might also be read as the pool of a small garden. In abstract juxtapositions of flat colors such as these the artist foreshadows at an early date the effects of the *papiers-découpés* that will crown his oeuvre in the 1950s. Notable is the freedom with which he treats the rectilinear contours of the window, producing, in effect, an unreal arch at the top. Such minor adjustments and dislocations serve to comment upon the rigidity of the picture frame, which is softened chiefly by the curving folds of the curtain, a feature that is itself held in check by the bold black strip that adjoins the picture frame only at the composition's base. While Matisse, like most of the Cubists, would never pass beyond the rendering of the world of appearances, he here touches a degree of abstraction that will not recur in his art until the monumental **The Snail** (page 127). In creating these master-pieces of representational understatement the artist does not seem to be posing a visual riddle, as is so often the case with Cubism and its aftermath. Rather, his statement is an unambiguous praise of color in its multitude of possible combinations. The viewer is drawn into a state of relaxation and euphoria through the means of the hues themselves, although a tenuous contact is maintained with the world of everyday, secular perception. In contrast with the intellectual challenge and mental tension provoked by such pictures as **Goldfish** (page 95), with their Cubist conundrums, the present picture is a model of decorative and compositional clarity.

Painted 1915–16
Oil on canvas, 57 1/4 x 44 1/4 in.
Florene M. Schoenborn-Samuel A. Marx Collection, New York

Goldfish

Of Matisse's several still-life subjects, few were more productive than that of goldfish. They occupy a position in his work of the early teens analogous to that of the reclining odalisque in the 1920s. The languorous, fluid bodies of these two motifs provoked, however, rather different pictorial results, given the successive stages of his development. This iconographic association is made explicit when the present picture is compared with similar subjects from Copenhagen (figure 16) and New York (figure 17), in which the round aquarium world of the goldfish is juxtaposed to a rendering of the bronze **Reclining Nude I** (figure 15), itself the sculpted version of **Blue Nude**, **Souvenir de Biskra** (figure 13) of the same year. And on the level of the unconscious, may we not see in this theme—the contrast between an aqueous and an atmospheric world—a marginal development of the motif of the Venus Anadyomene that is obvious in both versions of **Le Luxe**?

In the present version the fish in their round aquarium are placed on a table in front of a window in a curious, decoratively Cubistic manner, one which probably owes much to the artist's discussions and arguments with Juan Gris dating from the summer of 1914. From the strict Cubist point of view, the composition is not especially profound, and yet certain general tactics of his rivals' art are here rather naturally integrated into Matisse's more decorative approach, with its greater reliance on surface tensions. The space through the open window has been arbitrarily altered—interrupted by an inexplicable dislocation of what might be wall panels or window shutters, which are moved to the center, forming a dark vertical register. (There is a very remote possibility that the artist meant to indicate two windows of equal size, but this device would have no precedent in other works.) This type of composition employing contrasting vertical bands of differing hue or value turns up later in the final **Bathers by the River** (page 97), and this device, transformed into wedge-shaped areas of contrasting pigment, reappears in the two later versions of **Dance** (1931–33).

The theme of the view through the open window is an old and ongoing one in Matisse's art, but it is worth noting that it appeared in Juan Gris's **Still Life Before an Open Window**, contemporary with the present picture. Since it is a rather unusual work in Gris's oeuvre of the period, with an unusual (for him) overall dominance of blue, it seems fair to think that his painting is a reflection of an opposite current. In any case, in this quasi- or Neo-Cubist picture of a view through an open window Matisse has managed to indicate three separate environments, namely, reading from back to front: the sky of the exterior, the water of the aquarium, and the space of the interior.

PROFILE OF A WOMAN'S FACE (1960)
Courtesy of Christie's Images

THE theme of the painter and his model again surfaces throughout these later works. The model here is, of course, the last great love of his life, Jacqueline Roque, whom he quietly married in 1961, the year after this picture was completed. Her strong southern Mediterranean features are sharply profiled in a series of sphinx-like portraits. This work, continuing Picasso's lively interest in the imagery of antiquity, is similar to classical Egyptian representations of Queen Cleopatra with her enlarged, heavily kohl-lined eye.

The flat, planar approach of this painting, constructed from a few simple lines, is emphasized by Picasso's return to a tri-color scheme. Again, the polarizing force of red and green accents the lack of depth, throwing the profile into stronger relief. This technique was borrowed from Matisse and used to great effect with the Marie-Thérèse portraits of the 1930s, such as *Rest* (1932) in which the energy from the two horizontal bands of color stressed the stillness of the model lying asleep between them. Similarly, here, the whiteness of Jacqueline's face is lifted from the sea of intense green by the redness of the hat, resulting in a specific stress on the profile—and hence the picture's title.

Asleep (1932)
Courtesy of Christie's Images (see p. 128)

Painted 1916–17
Oil on canvas, 103 x 154 in.
Art Institute of Chicago

Bathers by the River

This painting, which began as the possible third decorative panel for Shchukin's Moscow stair, remained in the artist's studio for seven years before being completed in his Neo-Cubist manner. He did not completely paint out the figures that he had commenced in 1910, however, and this phenomenon is most apparent in the figure at the right. What seems clear from the surviving passages is that the figures were originally smaller, and that in the final painting they were enlarged so that they equal the entire height of the picture. Indeed, the figure at the right is so elongated that her feet are cut off by the bottom of the frame. A small project of about 1910 (figure 21) may reasonably be considered the original scheme for this monumental work. In this lyrical study we discover at least one figure, that farthest to the left, which derives from **Joy of Life**. The surroundings are relatively picturesque, with a waterfall heightening the effect of the river, which has virtually disappeared in the final version. In the completed work, the number of figures has been reduced from five to four. Matisse would never again model figures and objects in such an emphatically Cubist fashion.

This large composition leads into the much later versions of **Dance** (1931–33) in two important ways. First, it caused him to question the relationship of figure sizes to that of the canvas, with the result that while his early groups are almost never cut off by the frame—in fact, have much color area surrounding them—the ultimate versions of **Dance** permit the figures to stretch beyond the bounds of the arcuated frame in every case. Second, his use of strongly demarcated vertical registers in **Bathers by the River** led to the employment of wedge-shaped and diagonal color contrasts in the later **Dance**.

It seems that Matisse did not simply put **Bathers by the River** away in 1910, only to redo it entirely in 1916–17. A letter to Camoin of September 15, 1913, tells us that he had been working on his "grand tableau de baigneuses" in the course of that summer (Pierre Schneider, *Henri Matisse, exposition de centenaire*, p. 86). It is thus reasonable to think that parts of the present picture actually represent work done at that time, shortly after his visits to Tangier. In particular, the foliage of the leftmost register possesses qualities similar to his landscapes of that epoch, while the alternating dark and light vertical bands in the central and right portions suggest his manner of 1915 and later. If this is indeed the case, the artist's "failure" completely to obliterate traces of his earliest (1910) efforts is in effect a highly rational decision. It was his intention to terminate a canvas in which traces of his evolving style over a seven-year period would be manifest in a nonetheless totally unified image.

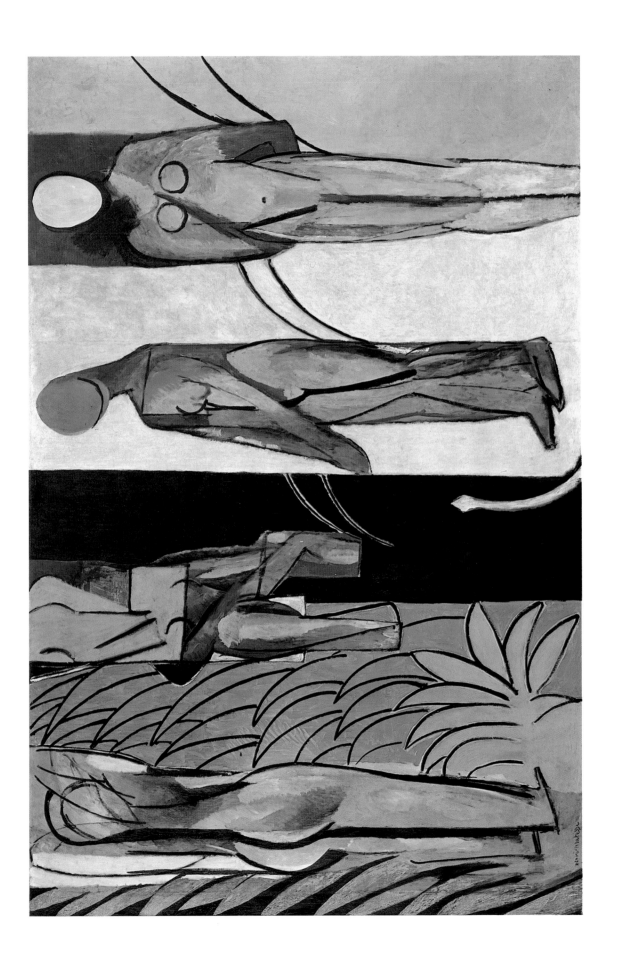

Painted 1916
Oil on canvas, 70 x 110 1/2 in.
The Museum of Modern Art, New York
Gift of Mr. and Mrs. Samuel A. Marx

The Moroccans

Matisse conceived this picture with all the deliberation and patience of a nineteenth-century academic master preparing a machine for some future official Salon. From the same letter to Camoin in which we learn of his efforts of 1913 on **Bathers by the River** (previous page), we learn that the concept of a definitive effort summing up his North African experiences was in the forefront of Matisse's mind. And despite the fact that his somewhat disruptive encounter with Cubism was occupying him at this period and is in evidence here, this remains one of his most totally satisfying large-scale works. The picture's novel tripartite division seems to break all possible laws of compositional order, and yet for Matisse it works perfectly. It is as if he were deliberately setting himself an impossible task of achieving overall unity, and then proceeding to accomplish it with apparent yet deceptive ease. It would seem that the black ground separating the three distinct parts, and also working itself into various areas of them, is the basis of his success.

The architecture of the upper left evokes **Entrance to the Kasbah** (page 89), and the display of melons and their leaves on what would seem to be the pavement of a public market is suggestive of the limpid, lyrical designs of **Moroccan Garden** (page 85), painted on his first trip to Tangier. These elements are situated one above the other on the left side. On the right we find a group of Moroccans at prayer, and this is the most challenging, hard-to-read part of the composition—in contrast to the forthright decorative simplicity of the opposite side. However, their gestures of supplication are somehow clarified by the design of the several melons in the lower left. As Alfred Barr points out (*Matisse*, p. 173), this area has been mistakenly identified as a group of figures touching their foreheads to the ground. The mistake is understandable because of the expressive abstractness of their design, and it seems quite within the realm of possibility that Matisse intended the ambiguity in order to clarify the more puzzling passages at the right. It is also a structural device that serves to link the otherwise fragmented composition, especially as the worshipers seem to be facing the melons and vice versa. The final unifying device is the repetition of the circular motif throughout the three elements, so that the domes of the architecture, the blue flowers in the pot, the spherical melons, and the rounded bodies of the worshipers all share the same motif. In this picture Matisse provides us with a distillation of his sensations, summing up his North African experiences much as **Dance** and **Music** (pages 73 and 75) concentrate all his efforts from **Joy of Life** on.

Painted 1916 (sometimes dated 1917)
Oil on canvas, 96 1/2 x 83 3/4 in.
The Museum of Modern Art, New York
Mrs. Simon Guggenheim Fund

The Piano Lesson

With its large areas of smoothly-brushed gray, green, and pink and its severely simple design, **The Piano Lesson** would seem to be the most abstract of Matisse's monumental canvases. Another version, **The Music Lesson** (figure 31), is of the same dimensions and palette but is more "realistic," richer in detail, number of figures, and atmospheric sensuousness. In general, experts have tended to place the Barnes painting slightly after the present version (actually the differing titles are a mere matter of convention, the two pictures being in effect variants of the same theme). Unlike the preparatory version of the Shchukin **Dance** or the earlier stage of **Le Luxe**, neither of these pictures would seem to be a study for the other. Instead, they are markedly different modes of handling the same subject and must be treated as absolute equals. One of the principal reasons for placing the Barnes version slightly later is the fact that Matisse's immediately succeeding stylistic evolution is toward a fuller, richer modeling and composition. The question is in any case slightly academic; what seems clearest in a confrontation of the two pictures is that the artist realized at a particular moment in his development that he had a choice of directions in which to proceed in his future work. By the end of his life in 1954 he had managed to explore both modes thoroughly, spending most of the 1920s developing a series of richly modeled, relatively illusionistic works, and turning to the more flattened, schematic mode only around 1930. Hence these two pictures sum up much of his work of the previous decade, and through this process of clarification foreshadow the two successive lines of his future development.

Painted 1917 (previously dated 1916)
Oil on canvas, 57 5/8 x 38 1/4 in.
Musée National d'Art Moderne, Paris

The Painter and His Model

This work, of relatively small dimensions when compared with **Red Studio** or **Pink Studio** (pages 77 and 79), was painted not at Issy but in Matisse's old studio on the Quai Saint-Michel. The most immediate reference for the present picture is **The Studio, Quai Saint-Michel** (figure 29), where the artist's chair is empty even though, as in **The Painter and His Model**, the work in progress as well as the model are present. Both pictures offer diagonal views through the window at the right, showing fragments of the Pont Saint-Michel and the buildings beyond, thereby evoking memories of scenes painted from this vantage point (including Notre-Dame) fifteen years earlier. The starkness of the figures and the setting here are in contrast to the luxuriance that is spelled out in the subsequent **Artist and His Model** (page 105), although one detail, the Moorish mirror frame at the top, will appear later in **Decorative Figure** (page 111), thus providing an incidental, anecdotal contact between this severe composition and the decorative profuseness of Matisse's subsequent work in the 1920s. The green of the model's robe and the purple of the chair are mirrored in the canvas on the easel. These strong accents are almost overwhelmed, however, by the relative absence of color elsewhere.

The design is almost as structurally contrived as the much earlier **Carmelina** (page 57), where the artist-model relationship is hinted at only through the mirror reflection of Matisse himself. One suspects that this is partly because both pictures were painted in the same locale; certainly it points to the artist's intimate, perceptive reactions to his immediate working surroundings. The pose of the artist is exceptionally rigid, almost that of an Old Kingdom Egyptian pharaoh, in contrast to the more comfortable position of the model. His body and palette are painted in a pale brown-orange; this hue is not meant to suggest a flesh tone but rather to establish a structural continuity between the angularity of body and the vertical of window jamb. The heart-shaped iron grille of the window—a variant of which we have just seen in **Goldfish** (page 95)—corresponds to the curves of the Moorish frame and relieves the picture's starkness. It is the theme of the picture within a picture, however, now shown with a temporal simultaneity absent in **Carmelina**, that gives this work its philosophical profundity. Canvas, mirror, and open window are here brought together in a thorough discussion of the art of perceiving and composing a picture.

Painted 1919
Oil on canvas, 23 5/8 x 28 3/4 in.
Collection Dr. and Mrs. Harry Bakwin, New York

The Artist and His Model

Coming in the wake of the 1917 **The Painter and His Model** (previous page), this gentle study would seem to indicate a slackening of intensity, a détente in which the artist gives himself over to hedonistic self-indulgence. Nothing could be further from the truth. The politics of the avant-garde, especially of the Dadaists, Surrealists, and Abstractionists of the 1920s and later, dictated that Matisse would be one of those painters castigated for having capitulated to a public willing to accept tame modernistic paintings, and for working for this market rather than plunging ahead into more obvious frontiers of visual and metaphysical speculation. But this essentially political criticism takes no account of Matisse's own private growth over the two previous decades (nor could these critics, of course, foresee where he would wind up three decades later). Hence this negative view is fundamentally irrelevant to Matisse's work and the necessity for a modification of his style at this crucial juncture. In terms of the inner coherence of his evolving career, Matisse pushed relentlessly onward all through the 1920s.

The design of this picture is complex yet sturdily ordered, and the nuances of color and tone demanded a supple, almost creamy texture to the paint, in opposition to the flat, sometimes indifferently brushed-in areas in some immediately preceding masterpieces. The break with Neo-Cubism, which had stiffened the structure of his large works of the period 1910–17 and which is immediately apparent in the contrasting versions of **The Music Lesson**, was necessary to further growth. The reduced size of his pictures during this period reflects not exhaustion but a change in environmental circumstances. He was working in small improvised studios set up in hotel rooms, rather than in the large permanent establishment at Issy or in his old Paris studio on the Quai Saint-Michel. The seductive outlining of the model here should be compared with that of **Carmelina** (page 57), and indicates a new and more intimate feeling for the natural, spontaneous poses of the female form. Matisse' is here in such possession of his painterly faculties that he can do without the arbitrary stiffness of conventional studio poses.

Painted c. 1925
Oil on canvas, 23 3/4 x 28 3/4 in.
The National Gallery of Art, Washington, D.C.
Chester Dale Collection

Still Life with Apples on Pink Cloth

Matisse's first painting, in 1890, was a still life (**Books and Candle**), and the theme ran through most of his career, frequently finding itself integrated into the larger interior studio pictures, notably **Still Life with Aubergines** (page 83) and **Interior at Nice** (page 109). Its ultimate metamorphosis would come in the grand **The Snail** (page 127). However, the painting of rather classical still life frequently enjoyed an existence of its own as a separate genre in his work. This radiantly beautiful study of yellow apples set against a pink cloth which reverberates with the blue of the background hanging is an exceptionally fine instance of the artist in mid-career, halfway between his beginnings and his culmination. Like many of the odalisques of this decade, this is a pivotal work both in style and subject; like the figure and interior studies, this painting shows the artist seeking an intimacy of scale and a compensatory reduction in overpowering architectonic design. The immediate sensuality of the image, the caress of the touch, are in contrast to pictures that come before and after. And yet this stage in Matisse's development is not inconsistent with the unity and the unfolding of his career. Here he seems to be reinvestigating some of the preoccupations of his youth, especially with respect to the Cézannesque disposition of the cloth and the way in which the fruit and pitcher are inserted into this arbitrary topography. Interestingly, there are few precedents for exactly this type of composition, with the angle of the table clearly facing the picture plane. Matisse's earlier still lifes, with the exception of the monumental **La Desserte** (figure 7), tended toward frontality. Clearly, at this juncture in his career he was seeking a new confrontation with the problem of constructing space in depth, using diverging lines of perspective rather than decorative framing devices and changes of scale. As for the resonant color harmonies, they grow from his long preoccupation with this problem. Here they are used to model forms rather than to create pictorial surface tensions. To a degree this preoccupation is contradictory to his goals as a Fauve and to the decorative, planar tendencies of his final works. But the investigations conducted in pictures of this type were a basic catalyst in the historical chemistry of Matisse's art; their role was to refine his sensibility and his proven accomplishments on a near-architectural scale.

Painted 1924
Oil on canvas, 39 3/4 x 32 in.
Private collection

Interior at Nice

Sometimes titled **Still Life with Raised Curtain**, certainly a more complete and focused description of the subject, this muted, sunlit interior provides a striking contrast to the monumental studio paintings of 1911. Once again the studio is empty of people, the model(s) dismissed. Only the artist is present, in a slight mirror image in the distance, visible just at the point where the curtain, employed to different effect in **Moorish Screen** (figure 33), has been gathered up. There the fully spread curtain served as a foil for the two conversing models; here it is employed with a Vermeer-like intent of providing a picture within a picture. The theme, which in Matisse's art dates from the mid–1890s and which, even then, was at least partly derived from his study of the Dutch *petits maîtres*, has never before been given to us with such graceful, nuanced clarity. Diagrammatically the composition is a reversal of Vermeer's **The Love Letter**. However, the light sources are complex: not only is there the light from the implied window at the left (whose panes cast their grid of shadows on the opposite wall at the right), but also the light from the window of the room in the distance, through which is framed still another view. It seems that Matisse never flagged in finding new variants of this key motif, a component of his repeated studio allegory. The still life in the foreground, consisting of a pineapple, some oranges and lemons, a flowered china bottle, and a vase of flowers, is set off by a red-and-white-striped cloth. Compared with the centerpiece of **Still Life with Aubergines** (page 83), this is another sort of luxurious opulence. The play of the yellow lemons against the bronze tray and the pale yellow-orange hues of the pineapple is indicative of the artist's refined sensibility in search of ever different adventures in color. The powerful, muscular color contrasts of the Fauve period here give way to a restful adagio of discreetly matched rather than opposed hues. Notable also is the way in which the vase is here outlined in white, whereas in paintings of a more intense palette black was sometimes used to support the structure of objects. There may be an overall sense of nostalgia in this picture, but there is no question of Matisse returning to an earlier style; there is nothing comparable to this painting, though much that is parallel, in the range of his earlier work.

Painted 1925 (formerly dated 1927)
Oil on canvas, 51 1/8 x 38 1/2 in.
Musée National d'Art Moderne, Paris

Decorative Figure (Figure Décoratif sur Fond Ornamental)

This is traditionally considered the culmination of Matisse's preoccupation with the female nude in an Oriental setting, and, in fact, a kind of turning away from his softer, more sensuous indulgence of the early 1920s. But the newly proposed earlier dating suggests a greater complexity (and even contradiction) to his various moves and strategies of the period. A charcoal study for this alternately stark and luxuriant painting exists (signed and dated—but incorrectly—1927) in which the pose is more relaxed, the left arm falling to the floor and the right leg more gracefully extended. Furthermore, the rendering of the form and flesh is more luminously suggestive in the drawing than in the final painting, where the modeling has become almost as schematic and constructive as that found in his work before 1920. The figure is the culmination of Matisse's Doric mode, begun with **Carmelina** (page 57) almost a quarter century earlier. That he could paint so stark a figure at this moment, while also producing others more diaphanous or more erotically fleshlike, demonstrates the control that he exercised during this period.

The background is a remarkable series of variations on a decorative theme, with a nominally repetitive motif that, as painted, never repeats itself in exactly the same fashion. Although the figure sits in stark contrast to the ever varying curves of this backdrop—which contains the Moorish mirror seen earlier in **The Painter and His Model** (page 103)—the drapery twined from behind her back across her thigh serves as the crucial link. The model sits within a grayish zone on the floor, which separates the patterns of the carpet from those of the wall. In addition there are a potted plant, a bowl of fruit, and, in the lower right, the suggestion of the corner of a veined-marble tabletop. Yet, in spite of this profusion of objects and motifs, the composition never seems cluttered; everything falls into place, even the abrupt, unnaturally straight line of the model's back. The tightly interlocked seated pose of the final figure suggests the later **Figure on the Beach** (1929) by Picasso, one of his eviscerated, bonelike constructions. Moreover, the complexities of this pose would seem to be the point of departure for Matisse's four *papiers-découpés*, the seated **Blue Nudes** of 1952 (figure 54).

Matisse's own comment on the frequency of this theme in his work of the 1920s is revealing: "As for odalisques, I had seen them in Morocco, and so was able to put them in my pictures back in France without playing make-believe" (Matisse to Tériade in "Matisse Speaks," *Art News Annual*, XXI, 1952, p. 62). It is especially interesting that he did not study these sheltered houris on the spot, but chose to reconstruct the image using professional models a decade later. The repeated creation of a Moroccan mise en scène in his Nice interiors indicates once again his propensity for constructing in his studio an artificial paradise, a perpetual invitation au voyage.

Painted 1926
Oil on canvas, 21¼ x 32 in.
National Gallery of Canada, Ottawa

Yellow Odalisque

The sumptuously modeled, opulently-colored reclining nudes, together with the odalisques in Moorish costume, represent as a group the artist's most revealing theme in the 1920s. They conjure up distant visions of similar paintings ranging

from Titian to Delacroix, rather than some fantasized yet minutely topographic view of the harem in the manner of Ingres (or some slightly prurient image out of Gérôme). For the most part it is clear that these women are occupants of the artist's own studio space, and in effect their presence serves to eroticize the objects from his own collections: screens, hangings, and so forth. Thus they further expand the theme of earthly paradise stated in the great mythological paintings earlier. But now the paradise has moved into the artist's improvised studio environment, functioning in a way not very different from the aubergines of his great tapestry-like composition of 1911 (page 83).

The present picture (there is a variant in the same hues but from a minutely different perspective in the Barnes Foundation) is one of the most robustly modeled of the odal-isques, which partly owe their inspiration to Matisse's several direct contacts with Renoir at Cagnes in 1918. It is notable that he did not pay much attention to this master's art until some two decades after his discovery of Cézanne, even though he may have seen Renoir's work at Vollard's around 1900. Matisse thus arrived at his comprehension of the latter's culminating figure studies after he had long since digested Cézanne's message and integrated it into the long evolution of his own figurative work. Hence, Matisse was maturely equipped, not to borrow from or submit to the influence of Renoir, but rather to clarify and intensify his late, classical-romantic study of the female form. Matisse integrated Renoir's individual mode into the natural course of his own increasing comprehension of the figure and its function in a painting. In particular, there were two paintings in Renoir's studio at the time which could have inspired Matisse: a partly disrobed Odalisque of about 1917 (Barnes Foundation, appropriately enough), and the double-figured nude painting **Rest After the Bath** (1919) in the Louvre.

It is noteworthy that there are relatively infrequent treat-ments of the reclining female figure in Matisse's art before the 1920s. The first of these, **Blue Nude, Souvenir de Biskra** (figure 13), is a post-Fauve work, a developed variant on one of the two central reclining figures in **Joy of Life**. The second is the nearly lifesize **Sleeping Nude** of about 1916 (figure 28), who with a few modifications could easily inhabit an environ-ment such as that of **Still Life with Aubergines**—this is, in fact, the picture that Matisse was working on when he painted **The Studio, Quai Saint-Michel** (figure 29). The series which the present painting represents thus relates to an earlier theme whose complete realization was postponed more than a decade, and its genealogy once more demonstrates the integrated continuity of Matisse's work and his ability as a mature artist of fifty to find stimulus in one of the great elder painters of the day.

Painted 1927
Oil on canvas, 24 x 19 3/4 in.
Collection Mr. and Mrs. William S. Paley, New York

Woman with a Veil (Portrait of Mlle. H.D.)

Portraits figure in large number in Matisse's work, and he was sufficiently attached to them to produce a luxurious album devoted to their reproduction at the end of his life (*Portraits par Henri Matisse*, published by André Sauret, Editions du Livre, Monte Carlo, 1954). The book is prefaced by a brief introduction by the artist himself. This ravishing picture is a portrait of the woman who served as the model for **Woman with Aquarium** (1921; Art Institute of Chicago), and whose features seem recognizable in other paintings of the 1920s. The rich, sonorous color of this intense study is an extreme statement of the artist's palette at the time. It is also worthy of comparison with the great Fauve portrait of his wife, **The Green Stripe** (page 61), where the color harmonies are in a totally different, more dissonant key. The structure of this starkly frontal pose suggests something of the angularity of the model in **Decorative Figure** (page 111). The woman's body seems enveloped in an enormous stole of a diagonal checkered pattern. The local colors, save for the flesh tones and the gray, diaphanous sleeves, seem to be largely of the artist's invention. The red, green, and yellow are close to the hues Matisse normally employed as a Fauve, but the atmosphere of the picture is transformed into something more luxuriant by the violets and pale blues of the background. The pose of the head, balanced on the model's hand, and the insistent relation of the body to the contour of the chair are suggestive of Ingres. Interestingly enough, in the next few years Matisse's art would offer increasing analogies to the work of this nineteenth-century academic master, notably in **Pink Nude** (figure 14) and **Lady in Blue** (figure 40). In his nudes and odalisques of the early 1920s, Matisse had already explored Renoir's ways of treating a classical theme. Now he turned, logically and methodically, to a rephrasing in his own manner of elements drawn from Ingres's even purer Neoclassicism. By turning in Ingres's direction at the end of the 1920s he was echoing a tendency that had emerged a decade earlier in the work of his greatest rival, Picasso. At the same time, this new influence in Matisse's art was completely consistent with his own inner development, and would shortly be revealed in the murals and the book designs of the early 1930s.

Painted 1930–31
Oil on canvas, each panel 12 5/8 x 34 in.
Musée Matisse, Nice-Cimiez

Studies for Dance I

The metamorphosis of the Shchukin **Dance** of 1910 (page 73) into the vast, expanded arabesques and athletic eroticism of the two versions of 1931–33 remains one of the most spectacular achievements of twentieth-century painting. Composed as a mural to fit an architecturally confining space in Dr. Barnes's main picture gallery, the commission provided Matisse with a new yet not wholly unfamiliar functional problem: **Dance** and **Music** (page 75) of 1910 had definite architectural ambitions (though they remained monumental easel paintings) since they were painted for specific locations in Shchukin's house. Moreover, the fact that Matisse was given erroneous dimensions for the lunette-like space they were to occupy offered the artist a second challenge to restudy the **Dance** motif, since the mistake was not discovered until one full-size version had been completed. He did not simply adapt his first composition to the new dimensions but instead reexplored the whole theme, emerging with an expressively different composition even though painted in the same hue and style. In the present preliminary studies, whose color concepts were rejected for the final versions, we glimpse the remains of the earlier concept of a ring of dancers, their hands held in powerful, linking tension. In fact, there are earlier studies (figure 42) that show this original motif, which first appeared in **Joy of Life**, virtually intact though intersected by the lines of the vault. Gradually the artist took this architectural feature into account, until in these present studies the tense circle is broken, some of the dancers having fallen to the ground in exhaustion while others remain erect, triumphant survivors of the bacchic frenzy.

In reaching his final concepts for the color scheme, Matisse had pinned large sheets of colored paper to the canvas until he found the appropriate solution. This was the first instance in the artist's work of the *papiers-découpés* technique, one which he would exploit more openly in the works of the last six years of his life. As for drawing the figures on the canvas itself, he also had recourse to a novel method. In spite of the many earlier studies and sketches, these smaller efforts were not transferred to the final canvas through the time-honored process of enlargement. Instead, he drew on the large canvas with a piece of charcoal fastened to a long bamboo stick, creating truly monumental forms while retaining intact the electric spontaneity of his innate skill as a draftsman in the definitive realizations of the project.

In effect it took more than three decades for these murals to find a totally appreciative audience, and the ultimate justification of Matisse's solution was helped by later achievements. Matisse's art here serves as the historic link between the mellifluous arabesque of a Neoclassic master like Ingres and the geometrically plotted curves of an abstractionist of the 1960s like Frank Stella.

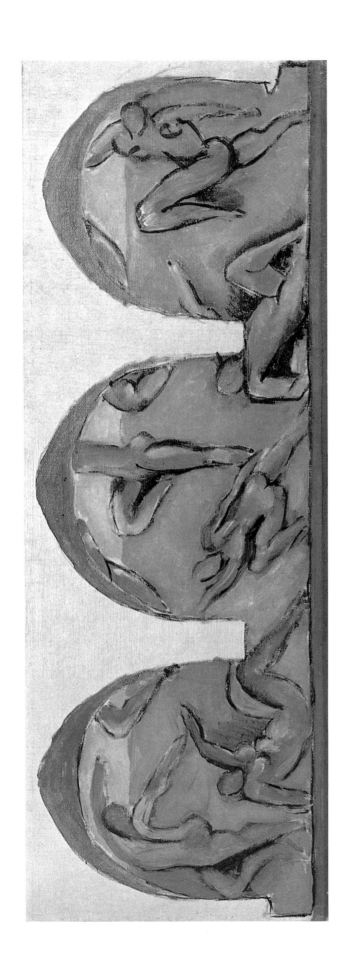

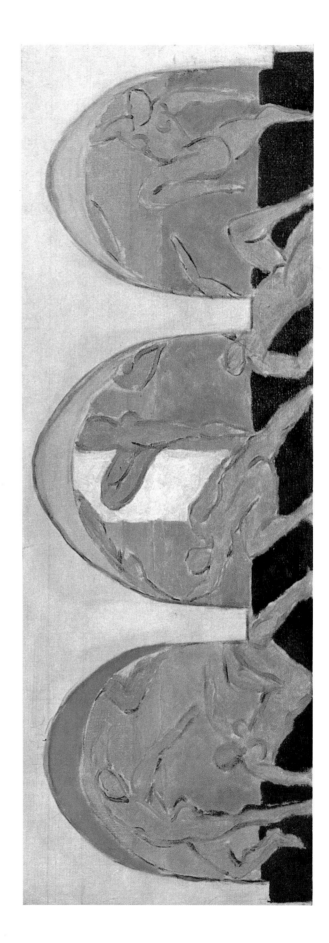

Window in Tahiti (Papeete, vue de la Fenêtre)

Painted 1935–36
Cartoon for tapestry, approx. 89 x 68 in.
Musée Matisse, Nice-Cimiez

During his visit to the South Seas, specifically Tahiti, Matisse did several remarkable drawings but no paintings. This was in 1930, just before he began work on the Barnes **Dance**. Hence it was not until five years after the trip that the artist sought to condense his experiences, relying in part on studies realized on the spot, producing this tapestry cartoon which functions as a monumental souvenir of his voyage. It serves to conclude a major theme in his art that begins with the development of the refrain of Baudelaire's *Invitation au voyage* in **Luxe, calme et volupté** (page 59). The several voyages, real and artistic, have now been completed, and for the first time in Matisse's art we can detect a valedictory note. Carrying over from the earlier picture is only the ship, moored with its sails furled. As we look through the open window across this placid, tranquil scene, the somber colors suggest a new and different sort of light in his work. However, here the theme of the open window is almost completely sublimated into the motif of the decorative border. Only the balustrade at the bottom suggests an architectural reference for the point of view from which the artist is recording his sensations. He had employed this decorative frame as early as **Still Life with Aubergines** (page 83), and it was originally part of another large, tapestry-like painting of 1936, **The Nymph in the Forest**, a picture that may well be a pendant for the present design.

Unlike **Luxe, calme et volupté**, here in **Window in Tahiti** the human figure has been banished, much as in the studio interiors of 1911. The foliage and clouds and the indications of a curtain on the left are of a curving pattern whose scale and weight is remarkably uniform throughout. One is reminded of certain of the Tangier landscapes of 1912, but now the design is firmer, more measured, more the result of reflection and meditation, whereas in the earlier tropical landscapes we are keenly aware of the artist trying to record, albeit in a stylized fashion, the immediacy of the scene before him. Much as with the Barnes version of **Dance**, Matisse has produced a composition summing up a continuity of experiences with the recurring motifs of his life's work. To a degree it is a less approachable painting than much that has gone before, but this Olympian attitude is understandable in the work of an artist at this point past his sixty-fifth birthday.

Painted 1939
Oil on canvas, 45¼ x 45¼ in.
Albright-Knox Art Gallery, Buffalo
Room of Contemporary Art Fund, 1940

Music

Two familiar motifs inherent in the art of Matisse are now distilled with marvelous restraint in another late masterpiece: that of the calming influence of music is here placed in the context of his repeated motif of the 1920s, a pair of female figures in either complementary or parallel attitudes. The female twosome was, in fact, the motif for some of his most splendid drawings of the Nice period. Later, this theme will be transformed once again in the 1947–48 series of women reading, but in the present picture the two women receive their most monumental, hieratic treatment.

As with many of Matisse's major compositions of this period, notably **Pink Nude** (figure 14), we possess photographs of progressive stages of this painting made while the artist worked out the problem of its design. In general these series of photographs indicate a progressive, logical, almost classicizing or archaizing process of simplification. He begins with a somewhat picturesque, even agitated series of poses, and gradually draws the whole together through a process of decorative rationalization. The original design of this **Music** resembled the contrasting poses of **The Conservatory** (figure 46), with the figures in even greater opposition. The completed picture rejects this idea in favor of a rather strict parallelism of pose between the two models, a challenging feat since they are so differently clothed. While there is no longer a specific indication of an Ingresque source in this design, as was the case with **Woman with a Veil** (page 115) or **Lady in Blue** (figure 40), it is clear that Matisse's rather personal transformations of Neoclassic design in the immediately preceding period made possible the present strictness and clarity of structure. And now we find, in the solidly outlined women, a suggestive analogy with his monumental nude compositions of the period bracketed by the two versions of **Le Luxe** (1907) and the original but subsequently overpainted concept of the **Bathers by the River** (page 97). Most likely this resemblance with respect to a massive outline was not a conscious procedure with the artist, but rather a spontaneous reintegration of an earlier device into his later style. This is simply one more thread between the past and present that demonstrates the surprising unity of Matisse's career as he explored so many different manners over the years.

Dominican Chapel of the Rosary, Vence

There is a temptation to see in this unique effort an exceptional, isolated incident in the artist's late career, an act of devotion on the part of an atheist, an ex-voto celebrating his recovery from the two serious surgical operations of 1941. Looking back over the artist's career, however, one is aware of keen architectural sensibilities on several levels. His repeated use from an early period of open windows or doors as a key constructive element in his compositions is but one indication; the great "Symphonic Interiors," environmental paintings in a strict sense, are another. The architectural ambitions of the Shchukin **Dance** and **Music** of 1910 (pages 73 and 75) have already been commented on, and the Barnes murals were considered by Matisse to be completely comprehensible only as an architectural fragment. Here at Vence he had his one opportunity to create a total environment drawing together most of the mediums in which he had already worked. That this, his only architectural project, should have come so late in life is one of the few tragedies of his career, for one can well imagine what might have grown from this tentative beginning.

The details surrounding the commissioning and construction of the chapel, which was built under the architectural supervision of Auguste Perret, are recounted in detail by Alfred Barr (*Matisse*, pp. 279–88). No paintings are present, the role of color being assumed by the stained-glass windows, which establish the interior tonality in such a way that the visitor, if alone, has the sensation of literally walking into one of the artist's paintings, especially one of the large studio interiors. The mural decorations, notably the stations of the cross, are in glazed ceramic tile—architecturally fixed drawings whose shapes Matisse pondered with his customary deliberation. He also modeled the altar crucifix and in addition designed the vestments for the priests. In this context it should be remembered that Matisse had previously, in 1937, designed the sets and costumes for a ballet, *Rouge et Noir*, for the Ballet Russe de Monte Carlo. Here, appropriately enough, the background motifs of the Barnes **Dance** (and even the architectural lunettes) reappear, his vast mural decorations thus lending themselves as a real-life setting for dancers on a stage. This effort must, paradoxically, be recognized as a precedent for the Vence chapel. In the end it is the blue and yellow of the windows and the magical nature of the light which they admit to the simple, functional interior that dominate the entire ensemble, ensuring its unity and establishing the chapel as a unique contribution to the history of contemporary architecture. Here at Vence, Matisse would seem to have definitively transformed the artist's studio—seen as a personal visionary earthly paradise—into a sacred place for others whose devotion took an institutional and even public character totally different from his own.

Painted 1952
Gouache on *papiers-découpé*, 115¼ x 152 in.
Musée National d'Art Moderne, Paris

The Sorrows of the King

This picture is in effect the last great essentially pictorial effort of the artist, a thorough valedictory summation and interweaving of many themes developed and repeated over the years. It is also a leave-taking, in which the artist (here seen as the king, shrouded in black, himself holding the guitar rather than his brushes) bids farewell to his studio, to his female models, and to the themes of music and dance. With a vivid and masterful blending and contrasting of blues, greens, magentas, and yellows, Matisse brings together many compelling, even competing elements in his art. The result is almost Biblical, with marginal suggestions of such themes as David or even of Lot and his daughters. The universality of this picture's eloquence is virtually unparalleled even in the greatest moments of his career of more than sixty years. Matisse is here able not only to draw together many previously unrelated features of his own art but also subtly to allude to certain of his predecessors and contemporaries without recourse to specific quotation; Delacroix and Picasso come quickest to mind. Its medium, the pre-painted sheets of paper cut out by the artist, almost as if the scissors were being used as a sculptor's tool, derives ultimately from the collages of Cubism as invented and perfected by Braque and Picasso a half century earlier. Here, in **The Sorrows of the King**, we have a symbolic collage, with the artist as self-recognized painter laureate. Color and design were Matisse's primary materials, and here they reach their ultimate apotheosis. Other works, marvels of his still-flowering genius, were to follow in the two years of life remaining, but as these images moved on into different realms of decoration and near abstraction, this picture remains his definitive farewell to his own unique, earthly past. It is a self-portrait of himself and his art, but a world removed from the realistic orientation of his 1900 canvas that serves as the frontispiece of this volume. Like massive bookends, these two pictures bracket Matisse's career.

Painted 1953
Gouache on *papiers-découpés*, 112 3/4 x 113 in.
Tate Gallery, London

The Snail
(L'Escargot)

The works of Matisse subsequent to **The Sorrows of the King** (previous page) form an interesting appendage to his career, one that points both to the possibilities of his own career going on indefinitely and also to the directions that later art would take beyond his own lifetime. In this fashion they incline frequently toward the abstract and even the transcendental. This composition of squarish and rectangular patches that organize themselves into a snail-like, spiral pattern has no precedent in his career. The tension between the angularity of the forms themselves and the imaginary receding curve which forms their unifying axis is a notable, totally unexpected effect. While it might be compared with the arabesques of the figures in the Barnes **Dance** and the way these are contrasted with their angular background, Matisse has here created a new synthesis. No doubt this picture will always be cited as a prototype for much larger-scale abstract painting of the 1960s. However, there would seem to be no individual artist who ever literally followed either this motif or technique, though several have in fact utilized its novel square format, one which Matisse and his contemporaries almost never used. An exception in Matisse's work is the **Music** of 1939 (page 121). With **The Snail**, Matisse was perhaps making a wry comment on Cubism (not so much as an art style as a journalistic slogan), but if this is the case it is only a minor component in the picture's underlying significance. Unlike many of his *papiers-découpés* of 1952–54, this seems not to be an architecturally oriented composition and remains a "picture." Hence its importance in the prehistory of present-day abstract art. However, in reaching toward a new world beyond the valedictory **The Sorrows of the King**, Matisse would seem to be proceeding toward a transcendental as well as abstract art. Since this square painting, conspicuously featuring squarish forms, is titled **The Snail**, it is fair to assume that the imaginary circular motif was of considerable importance in the virtually archetypal geometric forms here displayed. Considering that his final work, the abstract mandala design for a rose window in memory of Abby Aldrich Rockefeller (Union Church, Pocantico Hills, New York), is a form universally found in Western and Eastern religions, it seems fair to see in this penultimate abstraction, **The Snail**, an instinctive striving for a final symbol of unity and concord. With this picture and the subsequent window design, Matisse has in fact reached beyond the earthly limits of his own art. **The Snail** thus stands on the threshold of another kind of existence as well as on the brink of another kind of art, one that he could perhaps not foresee but toward whose aims he was reaching at his death. The various works of Ellsworth Kelly, Kenneth Noland, and Frank Stella are instances of how Matisse's ultimate insights would later be fulfilled.

H. matisse
53

Project manager: Samantha Topol
Designer: Martin Perrin
Production Manager: Maria Pia Gramaglia

Cover image: Henri Matisse; **Dance**, 1910
The Hermitage, Leningrad

ISBN 978-1-4351-1747-1

This 2009 edition published for Barnes & Noble, Inc.,
by arrangement with Harry N. Abrams, Inc.

Printed and bound in China
10 9 8 7 6 5 4 3 2 1

harry n. abrams, inc.
a subsidiary of La Martinière Groupe
115 West 18th Street
New York, NY 10011
www.hnabooks.com